BUTCH CASSIDY WAS HERE

BUTCH CASSIDY WAS HERE

HISTORIC INSCRIPTIONS OF THE COLORADO PLATEAU

James H. Knipmeyer

The University of Utah Press

Salt Lake City

© 2002 by The University of Utah Press
All rights reserved

 The Defiance House Man colophon is a
registered trademark of The University of
Utah Press. It is based upon a four-foot-tall Ancient Puebloan pictograph (late PIII) near Glen
Canyon, Utah

LIBRARY OF CONGRESS CATALOGING-IN-PUBLICATION DATA

Knipmeyer, James H., 1947–
    Butch Cassidy was here : historic inscriptions of
the Colorado plateau / James H. Knipmeyer.
        p. cm.
Includes bibliographical references and index.
    ISBN 0-87480-736-0 (pbk. : alk. paper)
    1. Colorado Plateau—Antiquities. 2. Historic
sites—Colorado Plateau. 3. Inscriptions—Colorado Plateau. 4. Colorado Plateau—History,
Local. 5. Colorado Plateau—Biography. I. Title.
    F788 .K64 2002
    978—dc21   2002007145

06 05 04 03 02

5 4 3 2 1   Printed on acid-free paper

This book is for
Fred, Gary, John, and Mike,
who kept "pushing" me.

Contents

Preface

THOUGH I HAVE LIVED IN THE MIDWEST all of my life, I first visited the Colorado Plateau region of southern Utah and northern Arizona during a family vacation in 1960. I became enthralled by the uniqueness and beauty of the area and have returned over forty times, driving, four-wheeling, hiking, and backpacking over as much of it as possible. After spending some time in the region I also developed a keen interest in the history of the canyons and plateaus. I have read anything and everything that pertains to the area and have now accumulated a library of over one thousand books and more than a thousand magazine and newspaper articles dealing with the region.

In my years of hiking and camping I would occasionally run across old, historic names and dates carved into and painted on the canyon walls and rock boulders. From my reading and studies I began to recognize some of the names of early explorers, prospectors, settlers, and travelers. However, upon subsequent inquiry with local residents or agencies such as the Bureau of Land Management and National Park Service, I found that very little attention or knowledge had been afforded these old inscriptions.

Therefore, I set the modest goal for myself of locating and photographing all of the old, historic inscriptions to be found in the Colorado Plateau region of southern Utah and northern Arizona, with the Mesa Verde area of southwestern Colorado included. Though I had taken some photographs in prior years, the summer of 1976 was the first time that I set out with the actual intent of recording old inscriptions. At that time I naively supposed that there might be some two or three hundred such inscriptions, and that it might take me four or five years to "collect" them all.

It is now over a quarter of a century later, and I have close to sixteen hundred inscription photos and know of at least one hundred more that I have not yet located and photographed. It has become an ongoing and seemingly never-ending project, but one of endless fascination. From the very start, however, I had to establish two sets of criteria: where and when.

The Colorado Plateau is one of the physiographic provinces of the North American continent delineated by geographers on the basis of its underlying geology and its visible landforms. As the term "plateau," from the French word for "tray," would suggest, the region is made up primarily of flat-lying, generally horizontal rock layers. Because of tectonic uplift, however, the resultant downcutting rivers and streams have dissected the landscape into a myriad of canyons and gorges, which now separate smaller plateaus, mesas, buttes, and, eventually, pinnacles.

This canyon-and-plateau province is roughly triangular in shape, extending downward from the Uinta Mountains of Utah, southwest to the Grand Wash Cliffs in Arizona, and southeast to the Chacra Mesa area of New Mexico. Generally speaking, this triangle is bounded on the east by the Rocky Mountain province, on the west by the Great Basin province, and on the south where the Mogollon Rim drops off to the desert region of the Basin and Range province. For my searches, however, and the scope of this book, I have restricted this vast region somewhat to Utah's Book Cliffs on the north, the High Plateaus of Utah on the west, the Mesa Verde area of Colorado to the southeast, and the Navajo country and Grand Canyon of Arizona on the south.

Perhaps more important was the time-frame. By the term "historic," I am referring to inscriptions that have been left utilizing a *written* language. This, by my definition, is in contrast to the "prehistoric" pictographs left by various Native American peoples. While many of these stylized "pictures" do convey information of various kinds, they do not use an established alphabet. Therefore, all of the hundreds of inscriptions that I have found in the Colorado Plateau region are of European-American origin, whether they be written in Spanish, French, English, or some other language.

Arbitrarily, obviously, I have established a cut-off date of A.D. 1900 for most of my inscriptions. By that time the vast majority of the Colorado Plateau had been visited and explored with very few exceptions. One of these, however, is covered in the concluding chapter of this book and contains the "latest" inscriptions included herein, dated 1909. This was geographically, and therefore historically, significant.

Let me state here that this book is not intended to be a detailed, all-inclusive history of the Colorado Plateau region. The history that has been provided is simply to put the various inscriptions in their historical context and to give a smoother flow, chronologically speaking, to the narrative.

Inscriptions have been both incised into and drawn onto rock surfaces. In the Colorado Plateau region I have found them lightly scratched, with perhaps a knifepoint or horseshoe nail, pecked in with some sort of metal tool, possibly a miner's pick, and sometimes carved deeply with a chisel. Some have been painted on with an actual pigment, but most of this type have been made with axle-grease from a wagon, wet charcoal, a fire-blackened stick, or even the lead of a bullet.

Three types of locations have, in the main, been utilized for the vast majority of historic inscriptions that I have found and photographed. The first is camping places, usually by or very close to a source of water. The second is either on or by an unusual or striking feature, such as a rock formation of some type or an archeological site like a pueblo ruin or cliff dwelling. The third is either on or easily visible from a route of travel.

The content of these historic inscriptions, of course, varies. Most are a name and a date, though many are simply a name or initials, while some contain only a date. Occasionally additional information is given: where those who made the inscriptions were from, where they were going, what they were doing, or what they had done. But all of them proclaim to the world in one form or another that "I was here. I am a part of history."

James H. Knipmeyer
July, 2001

Acknowledgments

MANY ARE THOSE WHO HAVE HELPED ME in one way or another with this project over the years. But first of all I would like to thank my late parents, Bill and Mary Knipmeyer, for first taking me "to Utah," and my brother, Bill, who accompanied me on my early trips there. And a special thanks to Mike Ford, long-time friend, fellow teacher, book collector, photographer, and hiking buddy, who has traveled with me to the Colorado Plateau region nearly every year since 1980.

Individually, I would like to acknowledge the assistance through the years of Fran Barnes, the late Bill Belknap, Fred Blackburn, Andy Christenson, the late C. Gregory Crampton, Joe Folgheraiter, Howard Hook, Bruce Hucko, Winston Hurst, Grant Johnson, Stan Jones, Wes Larsen, Harvey Leake, the late Dock Marston, Reed Martin, Dove Menkes, the late P. T. Reilly, John Richardson, the late Ward Roylance, Gus and Sandra Scott, Lee Swasey, Al Ward, John and Susette Weisheit, and Mitch Williams.

Dale Davidson, Bureau of Land Management; Doug Carithers and Nancy Coulam, both formerly of Canyonlands National Park; George Davidson, formerly of Capitol Reef National Park, and Lee Ann Kreutzer, Capitol Reef; Chris Coder and Colleen Hyde, Grand Canyon National Park; Michael Dussinger, formerly of Kaibab National Forest, and Connie Reid, Kaibab; Linda Martin, Mesa Verde National Park; Doug Crispin, formerly of Natural Bridges National Monument; John Loleit and Russ Bodnar, both formerly of Navajo National Monument; Richard Quartaroli, Northern Arizona University; Roy Webb, University of Utah; Gary Topping, formerly of the Utah State Historical Society; and Jack Burns, Zion National Park, have provided invaluable help for many years.

If I have forgotten and inadvertently failed to mention anyone, it is purely unintentional.

A word of thanks must certainly go to all of the staff of the University of Utah Press for making this book possible, including Marcelyn Ritchie, Rodger Reynolds, and especially Dawn Marano, my editor, whom I hope I have not caused too many problems. And thanks to Mr. David Catron, who, though no longer with the University of Utah Press, first approached me about doing such a book as this several years ago.

Finally, to my family: my wife, Bonnie, my son, Kurt, and my daughter, Kris. Thank you for allowing me to "go off to Utah" all of these times. I love you!

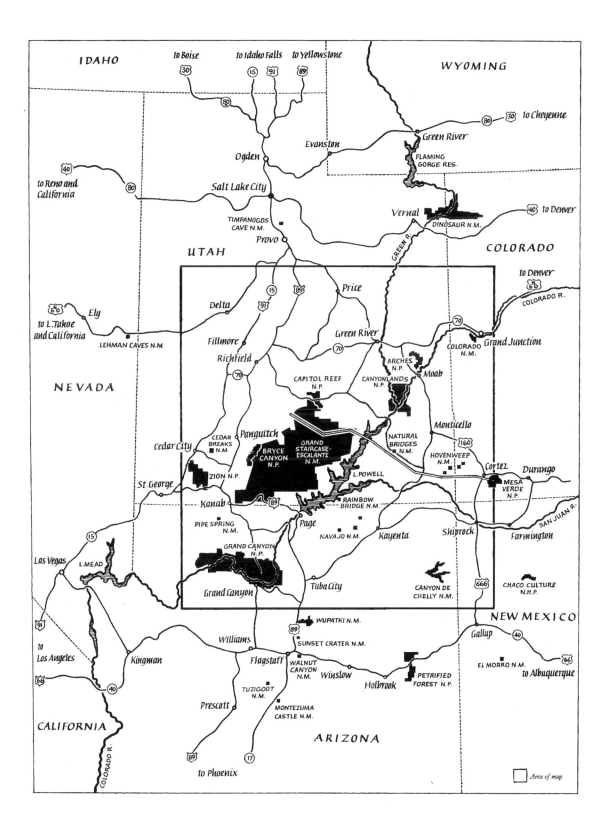

N
W E
S

0 10 20 30 40 50
Miles

*Denotes a feature flooded by Lake Powell

TAVAPUTS
BOOK
PLATEAU
VALLEY
• Price
CLIFFS
Price River
BOOK
CLIFFS
Grand Junction •
Colorado River
Gunnison River
WASATCH PLATEAU
• Huntington
Castle Dale •
CASTLE VALLEY
San Rafael River
Manti •
Ferron •
Green River •
Green River
• Moore
Emery •
Salina •
San Rafael Swell
SAN RAFAEL OR GREEN RIVER DESERT
ARCHES N.P.
Sigurd •
Richfield •
SAN RAFAEL REEF
CANYON-LANDS N.P.
• Moab
Dolores River
Muddy Cr.
LA SAL MTS.
Marysvale •
Rabbit Valley
CATHEDRAL VALLEY
THOUSAND LAKE MTN.
Dirty Devil River
★ Kane Springs
Old La Sal •
Fremont River
Caineville
Robbers Roost
THE MAZE
Beaver •
Loa •
Torrey •
CAPITOL REEF N.P.
Hanksville •
LANDS END PLAT.
LAND OF STANDING ROCKS
Dugout Ranch •
Junction •
Grover •
Fruita •
Notom
Capitol Gorge
NEEDLES
Circleville •
Pleasant Creek
North Wash
RIDGE
ABAJO OR BLUE MTS.
GREAT SAGE PLAIN
BOULDER MTN. AQUARIUS PLAT.
WATERPOCKET FOLD
HENRY MTS.
Cataract Canyon
Fremont Wash
• Boulder
• Hite
White Can
Monticello •
Parawan •
Escalante R.
Fort Moqui
NATURAL BRIDGES N.M.
BEARS EARS
GRAND GULCH PLATEAU
• Escalante
Lake Powell
Blanding •
Braffits Cr.
Panguitch •
PAUNSAUGUNT PLATEAU
GLEN CANYON
Moqui Canyon
Butler Wash
Cedar City •
East Fork Sevier R.
KAIPAROWITS PLAT. OR FIFTY-MILE MTN.
Halls Crossing
CLAY HILLS
COMB RIDGE
Tropic •
PINK CLIFFS
BRYCE CANYON N.P.
Henrieville •
Cannonville •
Paria R.
Hole-in-the-Rock
Grand Gulch
Montezuma Cr.
HOVENWEEP N.M.
Cortez •
ZION N.P.
ZION N.P.
WHITE CLIFFS
Kanab Cr.
MUSIC TEMPLE
San Juan River
McElmo Cr.
Bluff •
UTE MTN.
St. George & Santa Clara ←
VERMILION CLIFFS
Old Paria
Crossing of the Fathers
Copper Canyon
Aneth •
MESA VERDE N.P.
Mancos River
Virgin R.
Adairville •
RAINBOW BRIDGE N.M.
Olfeto Wash
Mexican Hat •
UTAH COLORADO
PIPE SPRING N.M.
Johnson Canyon
Glen Canyon Dam
NAVAJO MTN.
PIUTE MESA
MONUMENT VALLEY
MITCHELL BUTTE
MERRICK BUTTE
Four Corners
UTE MTN. T.P.
Kanab •
PARIA PLATEAU
TOWER BUTTE
ARIZONA
NEW MEXICO
Fredonia •
Lees Ferry
• Page
Navajo Cr.
Navajo Springs ★
KAIBAB PLATEAU
ARIZONA STRIP
Navajo Cr.
COMB
CARRIZO MTS.
KAIBITO PLATEAU
AGATHLA PEAK
Laguna Creek
Shiprock •
Inscription House •
NAVAJO N.M.
Keet Seel •
Rock Point •
Kaibito •
Beta-takin •
Marsh Pass
Chinle Cr.
CHUKSA MTS.
GRAND CANYON N.P.
WHITE MESA
Shonto •
Kayenta •
Chinle Valley
MARBLE CANYON
ECHO CLIFFS
Klethla Valley
BLACK MESA
CANYON DE CHELLY
Havasu Canyon
GRAND CANYON N.P.
Tonalea •
Pinon •
The Gap •
Tuba City •
Moenkopi Wash
Chinle •
Willow Springs ★
Moenkopi •
Little Colorado R.
Keams Canyon
Grand Canyon •
Hopi Villages
Cameron •
Steamboat •

UTAH
ARIZONA

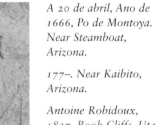

A 20 de abril, Ano de 1666, Po de Montoya. Near Steamboat, Arizona.

177–. Near Kaibito, Arizona.

Antoine Robidoux, 1837. Book Cliffs, Utah.

A. Cline, 1859. Long House ruin, Arizona.

J. W. Gunnison, 1844, J. Fremont. Near Moore, Utah.

J. D. Smith, 1844, R. M. F. T. Co. Caves Spring, Utah.

1st Regt. N. M. Vols., Aug. 13th, 1863, Col. C. Carson, Comn. Keams Canyon, Arizona.

I. M. Behunin, 1855. Ivie Creek canyon, Utah.

A. Mayhew, Pioneer To The Dirty Devil. San Rafael Swell, Utah.

J. Hamblin, June 15, 1865. Santa Clara, Utah.

F. S. Dellenbaugh, Jan. 25, 1873. C. R. Ex. Cave Lakes Canyon, Utah.

B. Beamer, 1891. Little Colorado River canyon, Arizona. Courtesy of Dove Menkes.

Miss Belle Kerby party names, July 12, 1899. Grand Canyon, Arizona. Courtesy of Mike S. Ford.

J. D. Lee, Dec. 25, 1871. House Rock Spring, Arizona.

Oh That Men Would Praise The Lord. . . . Willow Springs, Arizona.

Joseph Adams, From Kaysville To Arzonia And Busted On June 6, A.D. 1873. House Rock Spring, Arizona.

H. W. Lee, F' 75.
Montezuma Creek
canyon, Utah.

J. Smith, March 5, 1880.
Castle Ruin, Utah.

We Thank Thee Oh
God. Near Bluff, Utah.

M. A. Taylor, Oct. 26,
1890. Northwest of
Moab, Utah.

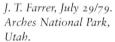
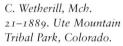

J. T. Farrer, July 29/79.
Arches National Park,
Utah.

M. S. Foote, Dec. 28th,
1881. Near Navajo
Mountain, Arizona.
Courtesy of A. W. "Gus"
Scott.

C. Wetherill, Mch.
21–1889. Ute Mountain
Tribal Park, Colorado.

D. Fairbanks,
T. T. Howe, San Juan
Gold. Capitol Reef
National Park, Utah.

Butch Cassidy. Capitol Reef National Park, Utah.

Monarch's Cave, 1892. Butler Wash, Utah.

H. French, 1/8/94. Grand Gulch area, Utah.

F. M. Brown . . . drowned July 10, 1889. . . . Grand Canyon National Park, Arizona. Courtesy of Mike S. Ford.

Col. Grand. Canyon. M. & Impt. Co. July 22, 1891. Canyonlands National Park, Utah.

D. Julien, 1836, 3 Mai. Hell Roaring Canyon, Utah.

G. F. Laughter, 1896. Canyonlands National Park.

The Worlds Greatest Natural Bridge . . . Rainbow Bridge National Monument, Utah. Photo by Kenneth L. Helfer.

ONE

A BEGINNING

9000 B.P.–A.D. 1538

From his earliest beginnings mankind has left inscriptions. We humans seem to have an innate desire to leave something of ourselves behind, to let those who come later know that "I was here."

It is generally agreed among archeologists and anthropologists that the North American continent was inhabited by at least twenty thousand years ago, with the temporary waning of the Ice Age's continental glaciers. More recent findings may even push this back closer to eighty thousand years before the present, but twenty thousand is an accepted minimum figure.

In the Colorado Plateau of the American Southwest, the earliest traces of human occupation, designated the Lithic cultural stage, have been dated as far back as 9000 B.P., that is, "before present." The later, so-called Formative, stage emerged by two thousand years ago. This latter included the familiar major regional variation known as the Anasazi, this name in the last few years being gradually replaced by the more "politically correct" Ancestral Pueblo. These people are well known to the general public for their aboveground structures of stone masonry, namely their mesa-top pueblos and canyon-side cliff dwellings, the most famous of which are to be found in Mesa Verde National Park in southwestern Colorado.

But the various subcultures of the old Anasazi are also known to a more select few for their rock art, which is divided into two main types, petroglyphs and pictographs. Just as with historic inscriptions, the petroglyphs were made by incising into the rock surface with some sort of tool, while the pictographs were produced by painting with various mineral pigments onto the rock's surface. Hundreds of sites containing rock art are found throughout the Colorado Plateau, the components of which cover a multitude of elements: human-like anthropomorphs, ghostly "ceremonial-being" figures, animals of various kinds, as well as abstract and geometric designs, and even simple lines and dots.

While in some instances the meaning of the rock art seems to be rather obvious, the true significance of much of it, though widely discussed and argued, is very little known or understood. One fairly common element of prehistoric rock art is the presence of handprints. At some sites there are but a few, while at others there are scores. Some researchers interpret such handprints, like most historic inscriptions, to be a kind of signature, a "signing," or census if you will, of the people living there. If so, these handprints, usually in pictographic form, would be a prehistoric example of an inscription.

These "signatures," however, are still pictorial in nature. They are not done in a written language using an established alphabet. The same may be said for another possible inscription from early times. In the Arizona State Museum in Tucson is a square-shaped slab of shaly sandstone covered with eight lines of hieroglyphic-like symbols. Found at a cave site in northeastern Arizona near the Four Corners, these markings have been related to the more modern characters of the Chinese alphabet by at least one author, who attributes the "inscription" to Oriental travelers around 2300 B.C.[1]

According to Henriette Mertz, and a few others before her, the *Shan Hai King*, the *Classic of Mountains and Seas,* was compiled in ancient China about 2250 B.C. and is considered by many geographers and historians as the world's oldest "Geography." In its Fourteenth Book, entitled "The Classic of the Great Eastern Waste," is described the "Great Luminous Canyon." Mertz, and a very few others, interpret the *Shan Hai King's* "Eastern Sea" as the modern-day Pacific Ocean, the land beyond as North America, the "Great Waste" as the desert-like regions of the American Great Basin and Colorado Plateau, and the "Great Luminous Canyon" as northern Arizona's famous Grand Canyon.[2]

Mertz implies that the stone slab from the cave in northeastern Arizona, with its "Chinese-like" symbols, is evidence of these early Oriental visits to North America. Most modern archeologists and historians, however, collectively dismiss such interpretations. Regardless, most epigraphers still identify the slab's symbols as "pictorial" rather than "written."

What may be the earliest written inscription found on the Colorado Plateau is located at a spring close to the southeastern corner of Navajo Mountain, on the state line separating Utah and Arizona. Here, in the summer of 1916, New York traveler and explorer George C. Fraser made a lunch stop at this ". . . water seep into a shallow dug well." In his journal he continues: "In the cliff is a shallow rock shelter 7 or 8 ft. deep and 10 to 12 ft. high, with picture writings made by daubing red sand on the white face of the rock."[3]

Fraser took two photographs of the picture writings, one of which is reproduced here. It shows pictographs and what appears to be an alphabetic inscription. In the early 1980s a transcription of the writing was sent to epigrapher Barry Fell, who promptly deemed it Iberic and gave a translation as follows: "Look! Fertile land terminating. Do not enter, it is desolate. This is I, Baha."[4]

Butch Cassidy Was Here

The ancient Iberians are believed to have migrated from northern Africa to the Iberian peninsula of modern-day Portugal and Spain between 4000 and 3500 B.C. According to Fell's theories, Iberic "colonists" came across the Atlantic Ocean to North America about 1500 to 1000 B.C., and he dates inscriptions left by these people from 1000 to 600 B.C. From man-made rock structures, words in Native American "Indian" languages, as well as written inscriptions, Fell proposes many various peoples of ancient Europe and Africa, Celts, Iberians, Libyans, Phoenicians, and more "modern" Norsemen, making numerous trading and colonizing voyages to the North American continent from as far back as 3400 B.C. up until A.D. 1400.

While Dr. Fell's studies and findings are not accepted by most conventional archeologists, it is rather intriguing to note that despite his having no knowledge of the inscription's location, his translation conforms well to the geography of the Navajo Mountain area. To the east is the wide, generally level expanse of the Rainbow Plateau, while to the west is some of the most rugged canyon country of the region, cut by the drainage of aptly named Forbidding Canyon. The description in the translation certainly fits the landscape, so it could very well be authentic.

TWO

THE SPANISH PERIOD

1539–1820

In 1519, with the blue waters of the Gulf of Mexico rippling behind them, the conquistadors of Hernan Cortes mounted their horses and started inland toward the Aztec empire of Montezuma. Within two years, the greater part of what is now the present-day country of Mexico was under Spanish rule.

Such was the beginning of the "modern" history of what would someday become the American Southwest. Just who was the first explorer to enter the canyon and plateau region is a matter of some conjecture. Interest in this region did not begin until 1528, with the tales of an Indian slave called Tejo. He told of going northward from New Spain (Mexico) with his father to trade brightly colored tropical-bird feathers for metallic and native mineral ornaments. They also brought back quantities of gold and silver and saw seven towns so large that they could be compared in size to Tenochtitlan (Mexico City) and its suburbs. These settlements were to be reached by traveling northward across a grassy desert for forty days.

One of the best-known ancient myths of medieval Europe had been that of the Seven Cities. Supposedly founded by seven Catholic bishops fleeing the advancing Islamic Moors several centuries earlier, these fabulously wealthy cities were first located on the mythical island of Antilla, somewhere to the west of the continent in the Atlantic Ocean. With Marco Polo's travels to China, they were shifted somewhere to the east. Finally, with the discovery (or rediscovery) of the New World by Christopher Columbus and the subjugation of the rich Aztec civilization by Cortes, a whole new continent lay open and waiting to be explored. With the Indian Tejo's story, the legendary Seven Cities now firmly implanted themselves to the north of the Spaniards.

Real interest in these unknown regions flared anew in 1536, when a group of four men struggled into the village of Culiacan. They and their leader, Alvar Nunez Cabeza de Vaca, were the sole survivors of an ill-fated expedition that in 1528 had landed on the west coast of Florida. For eight long years de Vaca, two companions, and Esteban, the Negro slave of one of the men, had painstakingly worked their way westward toward the Spanish settlements in New Spain.

In 1937 an old prospector who had been on the Colorado River in Glen Canyon, Utah, in 1894, reported having seen ". . . four signatures on the rock. They were quite blurred . . . and were long names . . . [he] remembered the name 'Alvar' and the date 1534."[1] However, in 1938 when a search was made, the spot where the inscription was purported to be was found buried by a landslide. Whether it was authentic or not cannot now, of course, be established. Historians who have attempted to recreate de Vaca's and his three companions' route do not put them within four hundred miles of the reported signatures.

But back in 1536, what caught the imaginations of the Spaniards were the stories that de Vaca and his fellow journeyers told. They reported that to the north were people who lived in large houses; cultivated crops in fertile valleys; made cotton clothing and worked in leather; and who had plentiful emeralds, turquoises, and pearls. Also, they said they had observed signs of gold, silver, iron, copper, and other valuable metals.

The first Europeans definitely known to have explored the region north of de Vaca's wanderings did so in 1539. Authority had finally been received from Spain to explore northward, and so there was organized a large expedition under the leadership of Francisco Vasquez de Coronado. But first he sent out a small exploring party under a Franciscan priest, Fray Marcos de Niza, to scout out the land.

De Niza, with the slave Esteban as guide, started out in March of 1539. However, he soon sent Esteban on ahead with a native es-

cort, to explore and report back to him if it was safe. Some time later, so the story goes, a messenger returned. To the north was a region called Cibola, in which were seven great cities with houses two, three, and four stories in height. All were decorated with turquoise, which was said to be abundant. It was reported to be thirty days' travel to the first of these cities, which was called Hawikuh, and was said to be the smallest of the seven.

De Niza immediately started off after Esteban. Fifteen days later, emerging at the northern edge of the desert, he received the news that Esteban and several of his party had been killed by the Hawikuh people. There has been a dispute among scholars and historians for centuries as to what happened next. De Niza said that he went on until he came within sight of the city, which he viewed from a distant vantage point. Pedro de Castenada, chronicler of the subsequent Coronado expedition, stated that de Niza returned to New Spain without going any nearer to Cibola than 180 miles.

In 1926 an inscription was found carved into a rock boulder just south of Phoenix, Arizona. Translated from the Spanish in which it is written, it reads, "Fray Marcos de Niza. Crown all New Mexico at [his] own expense, Year of 1539."[2] While a few

early historians accepted this as an authentic record of the de Niza party, modern scholars have almost without doubt declared it a forgery.

Researchers who have traced the padre's route place him no closer to modern Phoenix than 150 miles to the southeast. The wording of the inscription itself makes little sense. De Niza, a religious cleric, most certainly did not bear the expense of the expedition. The term "New Mexico" was not used until the 1560s and was not applied to the region of present-day New Mexico and Arizona until the 1580s. Upon study it was also found that the body of the inscription following the name, *except for the date,* is an exact rendering of the last portion of the Diego de Vargas 1692 inscription at El Morro (Inscription Rock) in New Mexico. It is now believed that de Niza did not leave the Phoenix inscription, but that it was made sometime after 1850 by someone who copied a portion of the Vargas inscription without understanding exactly what he was writing.

Back in 1539, de Niza reported that the city he saw was on a plain at the foot of a round hill, while Coronado the next year found it on the top of a low, flat mesa. De Niza also described the settlement as being larger than the City of Mexico. Once back

in New Spain and out of any danger, the friar said that Cibola was a land rich in gold, silver, and other wealth and that it had great cities. The houses were of stone, terraced like those of Mexico. The people were civilized. The cities were guarded with gates, and the people were very rich. In the country were gold- and silversmiths, blacksmiths, slaughterhouses, baths, sheep, and partridges.

In February of 1540, the exploring army under Coronado's command set off with de Niza as its guide. Four months later they finally arrived at the Zuni town of Hawikuh, in present-day New Mexico. What de Niza had termed larger than the City of Mexico was nothing more than an adobe-mud Indian pueblo. Coronado's report condemned that of de Niza made the previous year. "It now remains for me to tell about the Seven Cities, the kingdom and province of which the father provincial [de Niza] gave your lordship an account. To make a long story short, I can assure you that he has not told the truth in a single thing he said, for everything is the very opposite of what he related except to the names of the cities and the large stone houses."[3]

Coronado made his headquarters at the Zuni towns and began to consider if there might not be better things a little farther on.

Perhaps the reported gold of Cibola might actually exist in some other place. Therefore, in July he dispatched one of his captains, Pedro de Tovar, with an escort of cavalry to the land of Tusayan, of which he had heard much from the Cibolans. Traveling westward from Zuni, Tovar arrived at the Tusayan villages, the present-day Hopi pueblos of northeastern Arizona.

In 1946 a carved inscription was found and photographed at Steamboat Springs, Arizona. It reads, "El Tovar, 1541."[4] Though this and other nearby water sources are on the historic Spanish route from Santa Fe westward to the Hopi villages, the inscription was immediately pronounced a fake. Pedro de Tovar was never referred to as El Tovar, that designation not coming into use until 1905 with the completion of the famous hotel by that name at the South Rim of Grand Canyon. The date is also one year off; Tovar passed through this area in the summer of 1540.[5]

Tovar returned to Coronado with no encouragement as to gold or precious stones, but he did have one piece of information picked up from the Tusayans. Farther west there was a great river, and from reports it was navigable. It might represent the long-sought passage to the Western Sea.

Presented with another chance to save

his expedition, Coronado in August immediately sent another of his captains, Garcia Lopez de Cardenas, to explore this river. Cardenas and a party of twelve men soon arrived at Tusayan. From there, after a reported twenty days' travel (some historians believe that this figure is in error), they came upon the brink of what is now known as the Grand Canyon. Cardenas's party are the first Europeans, so far as is known, to view any of the canyon country of the Colorado Plateau. For three days they searched in vain for a way down to the river. On the fourth day three of the men tried to climb down the canyon walls to the stream. Late in the afternoon they returned, having gotten but a third of the way down. Cardenas finally gave up trying to follow the river and returned to Cibola by way of Tusayan.

After two years of futile searching and discouragement, Coronado and his army started back to New Spain. His report in 1543 was a disappointment. The expedition was generally considered a failure, having added no fabulous treasure or wealth to Spain. Coronado's inability to discover gold also put an end to any extensive exploration of the Colorado Plateau region of the American Southwest for nearly a century.

In 1598 Juan de Onate, having been chosen to head a colonizing expedition into the

El Tovar, 1541. Steamboat Springs, Arizona. Courtesy of the Southwest Museum, Los Angeles. Photo #P.4841.

north, led his group a short distance up the Rio Grande River into what is now the state of New Mexico, where they proceeded to establish a permanent colony. But even then Spanish influence did not extend very far beyond the narrow river valley. The country to the west and north, beyond the Zuni and Hopi villages, remained a mystery for many years. As one historian and writer succinctly put it, "The few who ventured into it usually did so only for a brief reconnaissance to prospect, to search for fabulous places, or to acquire geographical knowledge."[6]

Gradually, however, stories of a "blue mountain," somewhere to the west in what is now Arizona, were heard. The first reports of this Sierra Azul date from the middle of the seventeenth century. Its legend grew out of a confusion of various accounts of gold and silver mines and veins of "blue stone." Indeed, opposite the mouth of Lake Canyon, on the west side of the Colorado River in southern Utah, the date 1642 has been deeply carved into the surface of the rock with a metal tool.

The 1642 inscription, found by members of a river party in 1938,[7] is now covered by the waters of Lake Powell reservoir, but it had often been photographed before it was inundated. In 1945 another searcher discovered an old horseshoe nail in the sand di-

rectly below the 1642 date. It was square-shaped, not round as modern nails are, with its point worn off and bent at right angles. The bent point followed and exactly fit the bottom of the grooves of the "1642." Further search disclosed another historic inscription within twenty feet of the first, but hidden by brush. This carving reads, "C. Burt, 1896." Digging into the loose rock talus at the base of the cliff wall below this latter inscription brought to light an old rusted horseshoe, with the same type of nail in it as the bent one nearby.[8]

It is now believed that C. Burt, a Glen Canyon prospector in the 1890s, cut his name and the date in 1896. Then, evidently with a sense of humor and as a joke, he added "a really old date," 1642, close by.

From 1661 to 1664, Diego de Penalosa was the governor and captain-general of New Mexico. During his tenure he led at least one expedition into the country of the Cosninas (Havasupai) Indians west of the Hopi pueblo of Oraibi. He also planned an expedition to the Sierra del Azul, the ores of which supposedly had been assayed and found to be rich in gold and silver. Though the expedition was never made due to Apache conflicts and other obstacles, an inscription found scratched into the plastered wall of one of the rooms of an Anasazi cliff

dwelling ruin in far northern Arizona was for many years believed to have come from his time period.

This ruin is best known and received its name, Inscription House, from what appeared to be a name and a date. Most of the original inscription was almost illegible when it was found by an archeological party in 1909, but the date below was reported as being 1661.[9] That date would make it of Spanish origin, but years of search failed to uncover any documentary evidence of this early a visit.

At another cliff dwelling site in Navajo Canyon, no more than a mile from Inscription House, are a pair of perfectly clear carvings of two names, both with the accompanying date of 1861. It is now believed that these same persons, who were members of a party of Mormons under missionary Jacob Hamblin, inscribed the same date, 1861, on the wall of Inscription House, weathering having caused it to be misread all of these years. Modern photographic techniques, plus a detailed examination of early pictures of the nearly illegible inscription, have now rendered a generally accepted interpretation of "1861 Anno Domini."[10]

But faked, forged, lost, or destroyed, reports of old Spanish inscriptions in the Col-

orado Plateau region, like the legends of old Spanish mines, refuse to go away. A "Spanish cross" with a date of 1667 is reported to be in a remote canyon of the San Rafael Swell in southern Utah,[11] but a recent search turned up nothing, and local cattlemen have never seen it. Early ranchers in the Dry Fork Canyon area near Vernal, Utah, related stories of the date "Anno Domini 1669" along with the name Alvarez de Leon,[12] but again, recent searches have failed to find such an inscription.

The only authentic inscription reliably known from this early Spanish period is one found at Tuye Spring in northeastern Arizona on the established route between the Rio Grande pueblos and the Hopi villages. First reported and photographed by Navajo tribal historian and researcher Richard Van Valkenburgh in November of 1940,[13] it reads, "A 20 de abril, Ano de 1666, Po de Montoya." Van Valkenburgh and others since have tried to identify Senor Pedro de Montoya, but without success. The same name, without a date, however, is also found lightly scratched on the great rock headland of El Morro, not too many miles to the southeast in New Mexico.

By the 1680s it was not just the Sierra Azul, but rather contiguous quicksilver (mercury) mines, now inextricably bound up

"1661." Inscription House ruin, Arizona.

1861 Anno D. Inscription House ruin, Arizona. Courtesy of Albert Ward.

with the "blue mountain" legend, that attracted the attention of the Spanish authorities. A cheap source of quicksilver, used in separating the metallic silver from the crude ore, was greatly in demand at the time for working the mines of New Spain.

After the withdrawal of Spaniards from what is now New Mexico and Arizona during the great Pueblo Revolt of 1680, the area was left on a rather indefinite basis for the next twelve years, until in 1692 Diego de Vargas began reconquest of the region. The continuing Spanish interest in the legendary Sierra Azul played an important part in hastening the pacification of the lost area. But during the early 1700s there was never more than a handful of Spanish soldiers and settlers in New Mexico in comparison to the thousands of Native Americans. The Pueblo peoples spasmodically threatened revolt, and the "wild" tribes surrounding New Mexico were a constant danger. With the Utes and Comanches threatening from the north and northeast, the Hopi always an uncertainty to the west, and the Apaches constantly raiding in the south, there was little time to dream of new discoveries during the first half of the eighteenth century.

Sierra Azul was again talked about in reports by Franciscan missionaries who visited the Hopi villages between 1742 and 1745,

but after this time interest began to wane. However, if the Spaniards could not find precious metals, they then tried to accumulate wealth in barter for valuable animal furs. Though exploration of the northwestern frontier of New Mexico had moved slowly, about 1750 friendly relations were finally established with the Yuta (Ute) Indians. During the next twenty-five years Spanish traders, prospectors, and occasional missionaries explored the major tributary streams and drainages on the east side of the upper Colorado from the San Juan River to the present-day Gunnison.

In 1765 Juan Maria de Rivera, a veteran Spanish frontiersman, conducted two expeditions northwestward from New Mexico. In late June he took his party north as far as the Dolores River in what is now southwestern Colorado, and later in September as far as the Colorado River near the present town of Moab, Utah. From his descriptions, modern-day historians and geographers believe that Rivera and his party reached the Colorado either where the present highway crosses at Moab, or a few miles upstream at the mouth of Castle Valley.

At whichever location, Rivera did leave an inscription. In his diary entry for October 21, 1765, Rivera states that "I left . . . in a new growth of white oaks [cottonwoods], as a sign, a large cross with a 'Viva Jesus' at the head, my name and the year at the foot. . . ."[14] Obviously, no trace of this inscription remains today, as cottonwood trees do not live that long.

During the decade after the time of the Rivera expeditions, Spanish traders made frequent visits to the Utes, remaining with them, in some cases, two to four months at a time for the purpose of obtaining pelts. These expeditions, none of which were officially authorized, were probably few in number. Private individuals, some veterans of the Rivera expeditions, continued trading with the northern tribes. In 1775 three of Rivera's men got as far as the Gunnison River in western Colorado and possibly farther.

In July of 1776 an expedition led by two Franciscan padres, Francisco Atanasio Dominguez and Silvestre Velez de Escalante, left the capital city of Santa Fe to search for a route to the new Spanish mission at Monterey in California. Father Escalante believed that the easiest route lay to the north, and so it was in that direction that the expedition started. The small party was probably guided by Andres Muniz, one of Rivera's men from 1765 and also a member of the trip just a year earlier in 1775. They went from Santa Fe northward to the Utes in western Colorado, crossed the Colorado River just west of the present town of Grand Valley, then traversed the Tavaputs Plateau to the White River. Bearing northwest, the party finally came to the Green River not far below the foot of what is known today as Split Mountain Gorge. Camp was made on the east bank of the river, in a cottonwood grove a few miles north of the present town of Jensen, Utah.

In his diary entry for September 14, 1776, Escalante states that on the trunk of a "big black poplar [cottonwood] . . . Joaquin Lain dug out a small piece with an adze in the shape of a rectangular window, and with a chisel carved on it the inscription letters and numbers 'Year of 1776,' and lower down in a different hand 'Lain' with two crosses at the sides, the larger one above the inscription and the other one beneath it."[15] Like Rivera's tree-carved inscription eleven years earlier, this 1776 inscription can no longer be found today.

Fathers Dominguez and Escalante eventually reached Utah Lake, where they spent some time with the Utes living there, and then headed southwest along the Sevier River, keeping beside the western edge of the High Plateaus. It was now October, and concluding at this time that it would be impossible to cross the high Sierra passes to Monterey

before the winter snows set in, the expedition halted. The members cast lots, whereby it was determined to turn back to Santa Fe by way of the Hopi villages.

This decided, the two padres and their party continued southward to the Virgin River, finally turning back to the southeast along the base of the Vermilion Cliffs in what is now northern Arizona. Learning from local Paiute Indians that the great canyon of the Colorado River blocked any further passage in that direction, they stayed close to the cliffs, heading northeast to the area of present-day Kanab. They proceeded eastward through Nine-mile Valley to where a trail led them over the Kaibab Plateau to House Rock Valley. Descending the latter, they skirted the edge of the Paria Plateau, which finally brought them to the banks of the Colorado at present-day Lee's Ferry, Arizona. Unable to ford the river there, they climbed out onto the plateau to the north and headed upstream, searching for a place to cross. After twelve days they once again reached the river and the area that was later named Glen Canyon, and by following an Indian trail they finally found a practical ford. Ever since it has been known as El Vado de los Padres, the Crossing of the Fathers.

On the western approach to the ford some cryptic inscriptions have been incised into the sandstone of the canyon wall. No recognizable word appears, but there are several letters and they seem to have a "Spanish style" to them. Escalante's diary entry for November 7, 1776, when the party forded the river, makes no mention of any inscriptions, but they did spend most of that day in accomplishing their crossing. Indeed, at a point very close to the inscriptions, Escalante does describe the letting down by ropes of equipment from the top of the cliff to the bank below. There would have been ample time during that day for the inscriptions to have been made. First reported by a later Mexican trading expedition, which crossed there in 1829, they were even at that time inferred to have been ". . . made by the missionary fathers. . . ."[16]

From the river crossing the "missionary fathers" followed faint trails to the southeast across Navajo Canyon to the vicinity of present-day Kaibito, Arizona. Not far to the west, at what may have been Dominguez's and Escalante's November 12 camp, is another enigmatic inscription possibly left by the Spanish party. It was first reported by a U.S. Geological Survey group in 1884. Making camp there the night of November 16, Harry L. Baldwin noted in his diary: "I noticed on the bare rock an inscription, giving a Spanish name and the date . . . 1776."[17]

Unfortunately, all that remains today on the relatively soft, easily weathered sandstone is a deeply cut "17" and another more indistinct "7."

From there the Spaniards trekked south to the Hopi villages. The remainder of the journey, to Zuni and on to Santa Fe, had been traveled by them before. The Dominguez-Escalante expedition finally arrived back at their point of departure in February of 1777.

There seems to have been no direct trade with the Utah Utes prior to the Dominguez-Escalante expedition, but after they had explored a route into the Great Basin and had established friendly relations with the Timpanagos Utes in the vicinity of Utah Lake and the "bearded Yutas" along the Sevier River, Spanish traders began to push into that region. A local resident, writing about the San Rafael Swell area of southern Utah, stated that "near one tiny spring were inscribed a cross peculiar to the Spaniards, a Spanish name not understandable, and the date of 1777."[18] Another local historian and writer identifies this "tiny spring" as Tan Seep,[19] but a recent search of the area turned up no such inscription.

As early as 1778 a "bando" was issued by Spanish officials prohibiting New Mexico settlers from visiting the Utes for trade and barter. That the order was ineffectual and that unlicensed parties continued to visit the Ute country is evidenced by the number of infractions recorded in the Spanish archives. In 1812 a Spanish law was passed prohibiting Indian slavery, but again, this order seems to have been ignored by the traders of New Mexico. Because such trade was frequently clandestine and illegal, written accounts were seldom kept of the expeditions, and official records are largely silent on the matter. Only when laws were violated or trade was conducted without a license and the violator was brought to the courts do we get accounts and information in the records.

Circumstantial evidence gleaned from court documents from testimony given in a trial at Rio Arriba, New Mexico, in September of 1813, tells of one such trip. It concerned an illegal trading expedition to the Ute country, and indicates that it was by no means unique, and that trading ventures far into the interior country were frequent, if not regular, features of New Mexico life.

In June 1813, a company of seven Spanish traders, led by Mauricio Arze and Lagos Garcia, had left Abiquiu to trade with the Utes of the Utah Lake area. The reports say nothing about the first part of the route taken, doubtless because the trail was well known and had been previously used. From

Utah Lake they headed south to the "Rio Se-bero," today's Sevier River, and finally headed for home. Again the documents do not disclose the trail taken, but it is reported that the traders went to the crossing of the Colorado River where they found the "rancheria of Guasache" (Chief Wasatch), who was waiting there to trade with them "as was his custom." This would indicate a well-known and frequented crossing point on the river, but the exact location is not revealed. The river crossing at present-day Moab is hypothesized.

A few miles east of the little town of Moore, Utah, where Dry Wash and the present-day graded road cut down through the first upturned rock reefs of the San Rafael Swell, can be found the name "M. Arze." Unfortunately for historians, this in-scription is undoubtedly a fake, as evidenced by the accompanying date of "1812," one year too early.[20] Also, other names and later dates on the same rocky ledges are done in the same style and with the same red ochre pigment. Exactly the same names and dates are to be found in an early history written about Emery County,[21] and according to local "rumor," a county resident painted the historic names to show to some visiting dignitaries.

Though the region east of the Colorado River from the Gunnison on the north to the San Juan on the south, and the region west of the Colorado River around Utah Lake, seem to have become fairly well known by the Spaniards, the lower canyons, away from their headwaters, were poor sources of beaver and other fur-bearing animals, and the traders frequented the highland areas where the Indian tribes lived. The deeper canyon country remained unvisited and little known.

THREE

THE MEXICAN PERIOD

1821–1847

After several years of spasmodic revolt, Mexico finally gained its independence from Spain in 1821. In the latter part of the 1700s and the early 1800s, occasional Navajo Indian raiding parties had attacked the outlying Spanish settlements. Reprisal was usually in the form of limited forays to the west against the Navajo encampments in the Canyon Largo, Chaco Canyon, and Chuska Mountains region of northwestern New Mexico. After Mexican independence, the pattern continued.

Toward the end of 1822 a new governor was appointed to the province of New Mexico, Jose Antonio Vizcarra. In the summer of 1823, he organized and led a punitive expedition of some fifteen hundred troops to strike deep into the heart of the Navajo country, farther to the west than any conducted before this time. Beyond the forested Chuska Mountains, he and his men skirted the depths of Canyon de Chelly, crossed the barren Chinle Valley, and spent some two weeks searching for Navajos among the rolling uplands of Black Mesa in northern Arizona.

In the vicinity of today's Pinon trading post, in the center of Black Mesa, local Navajos had reported, sometime in the 1930s, some old inscriptions written in Spanish near a spring. The Navajos thought that they had been left there by a party of "Spanish or Mexicans." In 1939 a well-known Indian trader and a newspaperman friend searched for the reported records. Seeming to follow an increasingly frustrating pattern, they succeeded in locating the site of the old inscriptions, but found that a part of the cliff had fallen off and now covered them.[1]

Meanwhile, back in 1823, Vizcarra, upon learning that the Navajos had their main camp and flocks of sheep at a place farther to the north, divided his command. A detachment under Colonel Francisco Salazar descended from the mesa and made a base camp at "Cerro Elevado," probably today's Agathlan Peak. For two days his troops scouted the southern section of the Monument Valley area.

Vizcarra, in the meantime, traveled northwest, following Moencopi Wash through Blue Canyon. He turned up Cow Springs Wash and made a camp just north of present-day Tonalea, Arizona, at the two sandstone columns now known as the Elephant's Feet. The next day small parties searched nearby White Mesa. The second day they followed up Klethla Valley, through Marsh Pass, and finally encountered a band of Navajos near Skeleton Mesa. For the remainder of the day Vizcarra's troops pursued the Indians, probably down Oljato Wash, before finally turning back. The following morning the soldiers began their return trip, traveling to the Hopi villages and then back eastward to the mouth of Canyon de Chelly.

During this same period of time Salazar had searched north toward the San Juan River, but finding no sign of Navajos, he headed back southeast. Crossing the Chinle Valley, he rejoined the main command near the mouth of Canyon de Chelly. Vizcarra's recombined army then made its way back over its outward route to Santa Fe.

After Mexico had won its independence from Spain, the new republic greatly relaxed the restrictions on trade with the neighboring United States. Along with the traders and merchants from the United States came the fur trappers. Unlike the Spanish and Mexicans who obtained their peltry from the native tribes primarily through barter, the Americans went directly to the source and trapped the fur-bearing animals themselves. For the first two or three years they were evidently content to work the valley and tributaries of the Rio Grande, but by 1824 they were ranging farther afield.

In the spring of that year, Ewing Young, William Wolfskill, and Isaac Slover outfitted in Taos, New Mexico, for a pioneer trapping venture into the San Juan River area. According to one historian of the Southwestern fur trade, the three may have trapped far enough west along the San Juan to reach the deeper canyons, perhaps traveling as far as the Clay Hills Crossing–Piute Farms area. If this is true, then the trio were the first Americans to visit any of the canyon country of the Colorado Plateau.

On another trapping venture, in the fall of 1824, Thomas Smith and a French-American companion, Maurice LeDuc, are said to have returned from the upper reaches of the Green River by way of the rugged Utah canyon lands and the Navajo country. In 1826, a trapping party was reported by James O. Pattie to have ascended nearly the entire length of the Colorado River and its canyons. However, modern historians have voiced the theory that Pattie, and the group of which he was a member, actually went no farther eastward into the Grand Canyon region than the Meriwhitica–Spencer Canyon area. They then backtracked to the Virgin River, ascended it, and headed northeast across country to the Green and Colorado River area.

Also in 1826, in the early fall, Jedediah S. Smith led a party southwest from the Utah Lake region toward California. Smith had the twofold purpose of exploring for

new trapping areas and also to simply "see what lay beyond." On the cliff wall rising sheer above House Rock Spring in northern Arizona is the following carved inscription: "Jedediah Smith, Sep. 21." However, it does not have a year date with it.

According to the schedule developed by modern historians and geographers, and based on Smith's own account, his party would have been on the Virgin River at the Santa Clara, near today's St. George, Utah, on September 22. September 18 and 19 would have been taken up by travel "south two days" through Parowan and Cedar valleys, and September 20 spent in going up Ash Creek and down to the Virgin. September 21 would have been passed on the Virgin going to the Santa Clara River.[2] Therefore, Smith would not have been within ninety miles of House Rock Spring on that date. It is now believed that this inscription was probably left by one of the sons of Lot Smith, resident of Tuba City, Arizona, sometime in the 1880s.

In the summer of 1827, Richard Campbell led a party of men to California, going by way of the Zuni towns and arriving at San Diego in the fall. In later years Campbell remembered taking a northerly course, which went from Zuni northwest to the Hopi villages and on to the Colorado River

at the Crossing of the Fathers, which he described to Lieutenant James H. Simpson in 1848. They then headed west, keeping to the north of the Grand Canyon.[3]

On the east side of the Colorado, about forty-five river miles upstream from the Crossing of the Fathers, were (they are now under the waters of Lake Powell) a pair of towering fins of sandstone, called Register Rocks because of the several inscriptions left on the northern one by members of the so-called Hole-in-the-Rock expedition in 1880. This rock also contained one older inscription. Having the appearance of considerable age, it was not completely legible when it was photographed in the early 1960s. It read, "Dick T. Jo--in, 1827." Perhaps it had some connection with the Richard Campbell party.

By 1829 trips to California from New Mexico, and vice versa, were becoming a regular occurrence. Most parties traveled the southern route along the Gila River in southern Arizona, crossing the Colorado River at what is now Yuma, and then over the Mojave Desert to San Gabriel and the other mission settlements. But in the winter of 1830–31, a party led by William Wolfskill traveled northwest from Taos, crossed the Colorado and Green rivers, and then headed southwest. In the first portion of this part of

W. Wolfskill, 1830. Near Moore, Utah.

A W . L B, 1831. Near Paragonah, Utah. Used by permission, Utah State Historical Society, all rights reserved.

their journey their route would have been down through Castle Valley.[4]

On the eastern side of Castle Valley, along Dry Wash, can be found a now faint inscription reading, "W. Wolfskill, 1830." Within just a few feet are other historic names and dates, all done in the same style and in the same red ochre pigment. Most people, therefore, consider it to be spurious. (See Mauricio Arze, chapter 2.)

Wolfskill and his party then crossed over the high plateaus to the Virgin River and proceeded west to California. In western Utah the contiguous Parowan and Cedar Valleys separate the expanse of the Escalante Desert to the west from the rise of the Wasatch Plateau to the east. This served as a funnel for Wolfskill's route.

A mile or two south of the little town of Summit, Utah, named for the simple fact that it sits on the low divide between Parowan and Cedar Valleys, is Braffits Creek. In the early 1940s, two men, who were searching for prehistoric petroglyphs along the cliffs where the small but swift stream breaks out of the eastern plateau, found two inscriptions cut on nearby basaltic boulders. The first had a cross, the date 1831, and the letters "A W . L B." The other had the letters "T W" with the same date, 1831.[5]

It is possible that these inscriptions are a record of the Wolfskill party. There is no historical account of any other group being in that area at the time. However, none of the initials, if in fact that is what the letters represent, match up with any of the names of known members of the Wolfskill expedition. Though luckily often photographed after they were discovered, the boulders and inscriptions are no longer to be found. According to local residents, they were either destroyed during a flash flood of Braffits Creek or by a gravel business now operating at the locale.

It has been stated by many writers that Wolfskill opened the Spanish Trail for annual trade caravans to California, but there had probably been travel over it before this time. The route was called the "Old" Spanish Trail because it was believed to be simply a continuation of the trail followed by early Spanish traders in the latter part of the 1700s and during the early 1800s. Wolf-

*D. Julien, 16 Mai 1836.
Near Spring Canyon,
Utah.*

skill's route became known as the summer,
or northern variant, of the trail. The southern, or winter variant, had been traveled
partway by Dominguez and Escalante in
1776, and was completely traversed by Antonio Armijo the previous winter of
1829–30.

That the fur trappers gradually learned
much of the deeper canyon country is evident from the writings of Warren A. Ferris,
an employee of the American Fur Company,
who roamed the mountainous regions of
northeastern Utah and Wyoming from 1830
until 1835. He stated that the Colorado
River, a short distance below the junction of
the Green and Grand, entered a great
canyon, which he described as being in
many places more than a thousand feet deep
and bounded on both sides by sheer cliffs.
He knew that the river was confined in
canyons for two to three hundred miles. He
also had knowledge of the fact that its tributaries were also confined by cliffs for some
distance back, which forced caravans to
travel the more level plateaus far from the
main river.

Though Ferris himself did not see the
canyon country of southern Utah, he did
talk to and get his information from trappers who had. In 1834–35 he wintered on
Ashley Creek, near present-day Vernal,
Utah. Just before, he had spent several days
at Fort Uintah, a fur post on the Uinta River,
". . . occupied by those trappers from Taos
. . . ."[6] One of these men was Denis Julien,
who in 1836 made his way through the
deeper canyons at least from the upper
Green River in northeastern Utah to the
lower reaches of Cataract Canyon on the
Colorado. He left his name and the date
carved into the canyon walls in a number of
places.[7]

By 1836 the so-called "mountain men"
had been around the Colorado Plateau region for thirteen years. By that time literally
every stream, especially those in the high elevations, had been trapped out for their
beaver. Even in 1833 one of the literate trappers wrote that "These men [other trappers]
. . . were thinking about moving to some
other section of the country. There was a
large tract of land lying to the southwest
[the Colorado Plateau], which was said to
abound with beaver. . . ."[8] Julien was

perhaps scouting out the prospects of the deeper canyons when he left his various inscriptions along the Green and Colorado rivers.

In Glen Canyon on the Colorado River in southern Utah, is, or rather was, another inscription from this trapper era. Now covered by Lake Powell, it read, "Jan ce 1837," with what appeared to be a name, "V. Lay."[9] This name does not show up in any contemporary accounts or in historical records. Because the terminology of the inscription is suggestive of the French language, some historians believe that it may in some way be related to the Denis Julien trip of the previous year.

Yet another 1837 inscription, but inscribed eleven months later than the Glen Canyon one, is still to be seen along Westwater Creek, just before that stream breaks out of the Book Cliffs of eastern Utah. It is the name of trader Antoine Robidoux, and the rather lengthy message that follows, translated from the French in which it is written, says, "Passed here November 13, 1837, to establish a trading house on the River Green or Uinta."[10]

Antoine Robidoux, a French-American from St. Louis, Missouri, first came to New Mexico in 1824. In the fall of that year he led a trapping party far to the north from

Santa Fe into the Green River region of northeastern Utah. He eventually became a Mexican citizen and established fur trading posts near present-day Delta, Colorado, by 1828 and near Whiterocks, Utah, in 1832. From the Westwater inscription, it is believed that Robidoux also attempted a but short-lived trading house on the bank of the Green River, where the Uinta (now the Duchesne) flows into it from the northwest.

In the immediate vicinity of the 1837 Robidoux signature, as well as on the inscription rock itself, are several prehistoric pictographs and petroglyphs. There are also some historic Ute paintings. This was probably the spot described by an American traveler passing through the region on his way back to the Midwest from the Oregon country in the late summer of 1842. In the written account of his trip, Joseph Williams states that "The next night [August 2] we lay under the Picture Rock, and being sheltered from the rain, slept very comfortable."[11] Since his party was being accompanied by Robidoux from his Fort Uintah to his Fort Uncompahgre, they were more than likely following the regularly used route down Westwater Creek.

The year 1844 can be taken as the last "page" in the "account" of the fur trade of the Colorado Plateau region. In that year

Antoine Robidoux's Fort Uintah trading post was abandoned because of attacks by Ute Indians. A deeply carved inscription at a spring-formed cave in the highlands north of the Colorado River near Moab coincides with this event and can perhaps symbolically mark "the end" of this era. Here, in bold letters, is the name "J. D. Smith, 1844." Below are the letters "R. M. F. T. co."

These initials have been taken to stand for the Rocky Mountain Fur Trading Company, which was probably the most famous outfit of its kind operating in the Mountain West. Though it officially existed as an organization only during the first half of the 1830s, its owners and many of its employees were among the most recognized and well-known mountain men of the time. Even after its demise in 1834, many of its former trappers still continued to identify with it.[12] Perhaps that was the case of J. D. Smith, a "hanger-on" making a last-gasp attempt at the trapping trade.

FOUR

ENTER THE AMERICANS

1848–1864

Without getting into the whole idea of "Manifest Destiny" and the controversial subject of probable U.S. military provocation, let it simply be stated that upon being turned down by the Republic of Mexico in its offer to purchase the provinces of New Mexico and California in 1845, the United States declared war in May of 1846. By the end of the summer troops under Colonel Stephen Watts Kearny occupied Santa Fe and by fall were in control of California. The following year the environs of Mexico City itself were captured by a U.S. expeditionary force, which resulted in the Treaty of Guadalupe Hidalgo in February 1848. By its terms New Mexico and California were ceded to the United States.

As far as politically determined boundaries were concerned, the Colorado Plateau region had always been a part of New Mexico, whether under Spanish or Mexican rule. Following the Mexican War the newly acquired land in 1850 was partitioned. California became the 31st state, while New Mexico was divided into two territories, those of New Mexico (which also included present Arizona) and Utah (which also included present Nevada).

The new American officials in Santa Fe, both civil and military, almost immediately faced a perplexing dilemma. Their newly adopted Mexican citizenry demanded not only protection from Navajo raids, but also assurances that forces would be sent out to subdue the Navajo tribe. The Navajos, on the other hand, now also came under the protection of the United States and wanted Mexican raids on their encampments stopped. Simply put, the new territorial government just wanted both sides to leave each other alone. But habits cultivated over a century of time were difficult to overcome, and raids and reprisals on both sides continued.

Therefore, in the latter part of 1849, Lieutenant James H. Simpson and a contingent of soldiers and auxiliaries proceeded westward from Santa Fe with a twofold purpose: to chastise any hostile Navajos that they encountered and to conduct a council with those desiring peace. A treaty was duly signed near the present town of Chinle, Arizona, but like many an accord to come, it did not last. Raiding soon continued, and in 1851 Colonel Edwin V. Sumner led a military force into the reputed Navajo stronghold of Canyon de Chelly. But as had happened before, and would continue to happen in the future, it was more show and little effect. While the military expeditions in the new U.S. Territory of New Mexico were punitive in nature, others conducted in the equally new Territory of Utah, to the northwest, were more scientific in intent.

Now that California and the Southwest were part of the United States, and the nation stretched all the way from the Atlantic to the Pacific Oceans, the country began to press for the construction of a transcontinental railroad. Therefore, in 1853 Congress authorized four major expeditions to reconnoiter the most likely routes. The so-called "central route," which would pass through the Colorado Plateau region, was assigned to Captain John W. Gunnison. In the fall of 1853, Gunnison and his party of surveyors and scientists set out from Santa Fe, following the route of the Spanish Trail.

On October 1 they crossed the Green River and soon found the upthrust cliffs of the San Rafael Swell looming ahead of them. Since they were surveying for a railroad and not a pack-animal route, Gunnison left the trace of the Spanish Trail where it cut westward into the uplands. His party then looped around the Swell to the north and advanced back south through Castle Valley.[1]

Just within the first line of flanking cliffs on this west side of the San Rafael Swell is found printed the name "J. W. Gunnison." But there are two pronounced difficulties with this being an authentic record of the Gunnison expedition. First and foremost, it

is accompanied by a date of "1844," nine years too early. Secondly, it is in the cluster of historic names and dates, all done in the same style and in the same red ochre pigment, that have been described in the two preceding chapters.

Captain Gunnison and seven other members of the survey were later killed by Utah Indians when the party had proceeded westward into the valley of the Sevier River. Lieutenant E. G. Beckwith completed the reconnaissance the following year.

A scant three months after Gunnison's expedition came another, this time a private party led by John C. Fremont, a former officer in the U.S. Army. Having been passed over in favor of Gunnison to head the central route railroad survey, he and his influential father-in-law, Senator Thomas Hart Benton, decided to launch their own expedition, hoping to "show up" the official government party.

After fording the Colorado River at the regular Spanish Trail crossing near today's Moab, Utah, however, Fremont headed closer to straight west than had Gunnison, crossing the Green at the mouth of the San Rafael River and then following that stream on westward. Though the Spanish Trail route was obviously the best choice for a railroad grade, Fremont stubbornly refused

J. H., 1854, B. L.
San Rafael Swell, Utah.

to follow in Gunnison's footsteps. He attempted to force his way along the course of the San Rafael River, but was evidently forced back by impassable obstacles in the Upper Black Box beyond Mexican Mountain.

The map of the route, made by expedition cartographer F. W. Egloffstein, shows the San Rafael River and the surrounding terrain quite accurately to this point, proof that the party got at least this far. A few miles beyond, however, he represents the river as coming down from the northwest, by way of today's Buckhorn Draw,[2] while it actually swings up from the southwest. But the fact that Egloffstein evidently had knowledge of the Buckhorn Wash drainage seems to indicate that perhaps a few individuals of the expedition did explore that far.

Indeed, toward the upper end of Buckhorn Draw is a carved, very weathered, but still readable inscription, "J. H., 1854, B. L." Possibly these are the initials of two of Fremont's party. Unfortunately, no complete roster of the members of the expedition is now available for comparison purposes.

As described earlier and shown in the photograph included here, the name immediately below that of J. W. Gunnison, east of Moore, Utah, happens to be "J. Fremont." This, yet again, is one of the four spurious names and dates painted on the rocky ledges of Dry Wash Canyon by a local Emery County resident several decades ago. The same paragraph in the county history that the individual allegedly copied his information from mentions both Gunnison and Fremont, with a comment about an earlier expedition by Fremont in 1844.[3]

Daguerreotypes made by the 1853–54 expedition's artist and photographer, Solomon Carvalho, indicate that the party then followed the flank of the San Rafael Swell southward and west, paralleling the Moroni Slopes across Muddy Creek. Making their way through the rugged country of the Cathedral Valley area, they continued their westward path up and over the snow-covered heights of Thousand Lake Mountain before finally descending to the headwaters of the present Fremont River in Rabbit Valley.[4] It was now January of 1854, in the dead of winter, and here the expedition was forced to cache some of its equipment.

Sometime around 1950 a resident of the present-day town of Fremont, Utah, stated that as a youngster he and others often played in a clump of cottonwood trees nearby, and that on one of the larger trees was carved the name "John C. Fremont."[5] Obviously, this tree is no longer in existence today.

Butch Cassidy Was Here

From Rabbit Valley, Fremont and his party had to make a desperate, but successful, march through the deepening snows and freezing temperatures of the high plateaus to the sanctuary of the Mormon settlements farther to the west. In the northeastern corner of Iron County, Utah, the appropriately named Fremont Canyon comes down from the eastern heights. Near Sand Spring is a comparatively smooth wall of the canyon covered with historic inscriptions. One of these appears to read, "A. H., 1854." It is heavily weathered and the second numeral is not distinct, so the possibility exists that it could be a "9" rather than an "8." Again, without a complete roster of Fremont's 1854 expedition, it is impossible to try to match up the initials with a name.

The United States government knew, of course, that the Colorado River and its canyons neatly bisected the Colorado Plateau region from northeast to southwest. They had heard of it from both the resident New Mexicans and the early American fur men, but it had never been accurately mapped or studied scientifically. Consequently, two military expeditions were dispatched in an attempt to fill in this void, at least in part.

Early in 1858, Lieutenant Joseph C. Ives and a contingent of soldiers and scientists steamed up the Colorado River by boat as far as Las Vegas Wash, though he deemed the mouth of Black Canyon (now inundated by Lake Mohave) the practical head of river navigation. From the vicinity of today's Bullhead City, Arizona, Ives and his party then left the Colorado and headed overland. Guided by Hualapai Indians, they descended Peach Springs Canyon and finally reached the Colorado River once again at the mouth of Diamond Creek. Later, farther to the east, they also descended into the depths of Havasu Canyon, another tributary gorge of the Grand Canyon. Eventually crossing the Little Colorado River and visiting the Hopi pueblos, Ives and his party finally made their way back to Santa Fe.

In the summer of the following year, 1859, the second military expedition left Santa Fe. Commanded by Captain John N. Macomb, it too consisted both of army personnel and civilian scientists. Their approach to the Colorado River was at the upstream head, just the opposite of Ives's. In fact, their specific objective was to accurately map the location of the very beginning of that river at the junction of the Grand and Green rivers in today's southeastern Utah. Until 1921 that portion of today's Colorado River extending upstream from the mouth of the Green to its source in the state of Colorado was known as the Grand River.

A. H., 1854. Fremont Wash, Utah.

T. W. Walker,
Sept. 12, 1859. Long
House ruin, Arizona.

M. Murphy, 1859. Long
House ruin, Arizona.

The Macomb party basically followed the route of the old Spanish Trail from Santa Fe into the Dry Valley region of southeast Utah. From there they struck out northwest, eventually following the lower course of Indian Creek to a point not far from where it flowed into the Grand. Climbing out onto an elevated butte, they observed in the distance what they mistakenly identified as the junction of the Grand and the Green. Believing their objective to have been accomplished, Macomb and his group retraced their steps to Dry Valley and proceeded southward to the San Juan River. Following that stream back into New Mexico, they eventually arrived back at Santa Fe.

Relations between the Navajo tribe and the New Mexicans, both the older Hispanics and the more recent Americans, had not changed or improved during the decade of the 1850s. United States officials had succumbed to the misleading notion that when a Navajo headman signed a treaty he was doing so on behalf of the entire tribe, when in reality he was at most speaking only for his immediate band. Other bands in other parts of the Navajo country may not have even heard of the treaty, much less felt compelled to abide by its terms. So relations continued to deteriorate. In fact, in 1851, following Colonel Sumner's ineffectual foray

into the depths of Canyon de Chelly, a military post, Fort Defiance, was established in what is now far northeastern Arizona.

In September of 1859, a detachment of troops under the command of Captain John G. Walker left Fort Defiance on a reconnaissance to the western Navajo country and into regions never before visited by American troops. Like Vizcarra thirty-six years earlier, Walker's force skirted Canyon de Chelly, crossed the Chinle Valley, and climbed Black Mesa. Following the mesa's rim, they came to a point three or four miles west of Marsh Pass, overlooking the head of Klethla Valley. Descending the mesa by a precipitous trail, the detachment camped the night of September 12 at an old pueblo ruin.[6]

This ruin is the prehistoric Anasazi structure known today as Long House. While camped at the foot of the rounded knoll on which the ruined pueblo sits, several members of Walker's troop, including the captain himself, found the time to walk up to its still-standing walls and engrave their names and the date into the stone building blocks. From lists made beginning in the 1920s, no fewer than thirteen inscriptions were left by the Walker detachment, ten of which are still completely or partially readable.

A. Cline, S. J. M., J. Douglas, T. W. Walker, and M. Murphy gave only their

names and the date. W. Callaghan, W.
Bracken, Hugh Bailey, C. G. H., Lieutenant
W. H. Bell, Kaiser, and Captain Walker included the information that they were from
Company G, 3rd Infantry. Lieutenant Bell
and Captain Walker also added "U. S. A.,"
undoubtedly signifying U.S. Army rather
than United States of America. Lastly, one
inscription, unsigned, is the general statement, "Visited by Capt. Walker's Command
of Mtd. [Mounted] Rifles & 3d. Inf., Sept.
12th, 1859."

The next day the command traveled eastward through Marsh Pass and past the
mouth of Tsegi Canyon. From this point the
troop's path led along the northeastern foot
of Black Mesa, back across the Chinle Valley, and then south of Canyon de Chelly to
Fort Defiance.

One year later, in October of 1860, and

acting, no doubt, at least in part from the
Walker reconnaissance, a major military expedition was launched against the western Navajos. A sizable force under the command of
Colonel Edward R. S. Canby marched back
over Walker's route, intending to trap fleeing
bands of hostiles in the supposedly pinched-off
angle between the bulk of Black Mesa on the
south and the Sierra Limitas (today's Tsegi
mesas) on the north. Using the now usual
route west from Fort Defiance, Canby's
columns then followed Chinle Wash northward. They paused for a break sometime early
in the afternoon of October 21, at a point
about four miles northwest of present-day
Rock Point, Arizona. In his subsequent report
at the conclusion of the expedition, second-in-
command Major Henry H. Sibley mentions in
his entry for the 21st, ". . . further on beside
the trail are curious Indian inscriptions—."[7]

*C. B. Brady,
2nd Dragoons,
October 21st, 1860.
Near Rock Point,
Arizona.*

*Blas Lucero, ano de
1860. Near Rock Point,
Arizona.*

There are scores, if not hundreds, of pre-historic petroglyphs incised into the vertical faces of two large sandstone outcroppings on the west side of Chinle Wash. The Navajos called them Big and Little Talking Rocks, assuming that the ancient markings were some sort of message or information. The rocks attracted the attention not only of Major Sibley, but at least three of his men as well. Among the petroglyphs C. B. Brady inscribed his name and the date, "October 21st, 1860." Blas Lucero, the "captain" of a group of twenty "guides" (volunteer merce-naries), carved his name and the year date. One unnamed person simply left the general inscription, "Navajoe [sic] expedition, October 21st, 1860."

But a short distance to the north, Canby's troops turned westward along the base of Black Mesa to Laguna Creek. Following up that stream they came to what they called "Canon Limitar," today's Marsh Pass–Tsegi Canyon area, and established a camp three or four miles up the latter. During the next four days Canby sent out various companies of soldiers to search the surrounding canyons and mesas.[8] One of these companies that must have been dispatched to the southwest into the Klethla Valley area was under the command of Captain Henry R. Selden. Stops may have been made at

Long House ruin both going and returning, as Captain Selden left his name and the date there twice, both indicating October 26.

Fruitless searches for Navajo bands to engage in direct combat proved to Canby the incorrectness of the theory that any flee-ing hostiles would be trapped by the topog-raphy of the region. By the beginning of No-vember he and his forces were on the march back to Fort Defiance.

Military events in the Colorado Plateau region were now suspended by the eruption of the Civil War back in the East in 1861 and the unsuccessful Confederate attempt to gain control of New Mexico Territory in 1862. But now it was time to once again face the problem of Apache, Comanche, and Navajo raids on New Mexico settlements, which had increased anew with the interrup-tion of the War Between the States. In the spring of 1863, Colonel Christopher "Kit" Carson was given command of the Navajo portion of the campaign. The plan of his su-periors in Santa Fe was to engage in a "scorched earth" policy. Throughout the summer and fall Navajo livestock was to be captured or killed, crops destroyed, and hogans (houses) burned.

One such foray was led by Carson from the re-established Fort Defiance in August. They marched westward toward the Hopi

villages, camping the nights of the 12th, 13th, and 14th in what was later called Keams Canyon. In his entry for the 14th, Captain Eben Everett, commanding officer of Company B, noted in his diary: "One of our men was yesterday at work chiseling in the face of a smooth rock on the side of the canyon [a] legend . . . in letters a foot square."[9] This inscription may still be clearly seen today, a couple of miles up canyon from the present Keams Canyon trading post. It reads, "1st Regt. N. M. Vols., Aug 13th, 1863, Col. C. Carson, Comn."

After leaving their Keams Canyon camp, Carson's regiment of New Mexico volunteers made their way back eastward to the vicinity of Ganado. From there they traveled northward to the area around Chinle and the mouth of Canyon de Chelly before finally returning to Fort Defiance.

Early in January 1864, Carson was directed to make a sweep through the Navajo stronghold of Canyon de Chelly itself. The force consisted of two columns. One, led by Carson, would block the entrance to the canyon at its western end. The other column, commanded by Captain Albert H. Pfeiffer, would march down the canyon, sup-

posedly trapping the Navajo between them. In his subsequent written report, Pfeiffer stated, "On the 12th inst . . . I encamped that evening in a secure place. . . ."[10]

The location of this camp was at the mouth of a tributary gorge called Many Cherry Canyon. During a rock art survey in the early 1970s, a dim inscription was found carved into the sandstone of the canyon wall.[11] Translated from the Spanish it says, "Jose Pena, C H 1 N.M.V. [Company H, 1st New Mexico Volunteers], Passed the 13th day, AD [Anno Domini]—January of 1864." Pena was obviously one of the New Mexican volunteers under Captain Pfeiffer and evidently cut the inscription the following morning.

The scorched-earth policy, plus Carson's penetration of their ancient stronghold, broke the morale of the now destitute Navajo and triggered mass surrenders. The conflict virtually ended at this point. Few Navajos had been killed, but the campaign to destroy and eliminate their means of sustenance had succeeded beyond all expectations. Over a century and a half of frontier fighting had accomplished nothing. Now it was all over in a few short months.

Capt. Selden, Oct. 26, 1860. Long House ruin, Arizona.

Jose Pena, 1864. Canyon del Muerto, Arizona.

FIVE

MORMON EXPANSION

1847–1868

While the Mexican War was taking place to the south of the Colorado Plateau region, equally important events, as far as the history of the area was concerned, were taking place to the north. In 1846, after years of religious persecution in Ohio, Missouri, and finally Illinois, the Mormons, the followers of the Church of Jesus Christ of Latter-day Saints, determined to move west into what was then Mexican territory. Led by Brigham Young, the first groups reached the valley of the Great Salt Lake in July of 1847. There, outside of the influence of the United States and in a region most considered desert-like and uninhabitable, the Mormon people believed they would be free to follow their religion and beliefs unmolested.

Little did the new settlers realize that only one year later the entire Southwest would be ceded to the United States from Mexico. In 1849 the Mormon people established their own State of Deseret and sent a delegate to the U.S. Congress to ask for admission to the Union. Congress refused it as a state but in 1850 did establish the region as the Territory of Utah with Brigham Young, president of the Church of Jesus Christ, as its first governor.

Within two years of first entering the Great Salt Lake Valley, several thousand Mormon immigrants now had arrived. Ex-

pansion was absolutely necessary, and to secure intelligent information reconnoitering parties were sent out in various directions to look over the surrounding country. In the winter of 1849 Parley P. Pratt was directed to lead the so-called Southern Exploring Expedition into the area of the present-day Utah counties of Iron and Washington.

Heading south past Utah Lake, the company crossed over to the Sevier River and proceeded to follow it to the southwest. Just as John C. Fremont's party would do five years later, the Pratt expedition left the Sevier River southwest of today's Circleville, Utah, crossed the high plateau, and descended to the west by way of Fremont Wash to the Great Basin. And just as Fremont perhaps did in January of 1854, Pratt and his group paused near Sand Spring.

In his diary entry for December 21, 1849, John C. Armstrong, a member of the Southern Exploring Expedition, wrote, ". . . one fourth mile farther there was a range of stupendous rocks . . . I cut my name on the face of these rocks. . . ."[1] Chiseled deeply into the stone, the large letters reading, "J. C. Armstrong, 1849," can still be easily seen today. Pratt and his party then explored southwest as far as modern St. George, Utah, before returning to Salt Lake City.

Subsequently, the towns of Parowan and

Cedar City were founded in 1851 and 1852.
As a result of the so-called Walker War,
named after a principal chief of the Utes,
Fort Harmony was established in 1853. To
win and keep the good faith of the Paiute
bands in the southwest, a group of Mormon
missionaries left the fort in the summer of
1854 to labor among the natives of the
Santa Clara Creek area, a tributary of the
Virgin River. This was the basis for the
Southern Indian Mission and the eventual
town of Santa Clara.[2]

On the rocky wall of Santa Clara Canyon,
along an old trail connecting the rim and bottom of the gorge, is a carved inscription. It
reads, "A. P. Hardy, June 15, 1854." Augustus P. Hardy was a member of this initial missionary group that spent several weeks that
summer among the Tontaguint band.

The warm climate of the Virgin River
area was found to be conducive to the growing of cotton, important to the Mormon
people for the manufacture of clothing. As a
result a new settlement was directed to be
established on the Virgin River in 1857,
which became the town of Washington,
Utah. Encouraged, but not fully satisfied by
the results, in the spring of 1858 Brigham
Young fitted out a small party to erect an
experimental cotton farm about nine miles
downstream from Washington.[3]

Today, a good pair of eyes from the highway below can pick out a rather detailed
carving high up on the rocky wall bordering
the west side of the Virgin River. It is an incised rendering of a cotton plant, including
stem, leaves, cotton balls, and roots. In
smaller letters to one side is the name
"Jacob Peart, Jr." That he was one of the
party instructed to establish the experimental cotton farm is indicated by the additional
carved message, "I was se[n]t her[e] to
rais[e] cotten [sic] March 1858."

In the next several years Mormon settlement steadily progressed upstream along the
Virgin River, with at least seven different
towns being founded. Even Mukuntuweap
Canyon, later renamed Zion Canyon, on the
North Fork of the Virgin, was eventually
settled by familes in 1865. On the East Fork,
not far within Parunuweap Canyon, the tiny

*J. C. Armstrong, 1849.
Fremont Wash, Utah.*

*A. P. Hardy,
June 15, 1854. Near
Santa Clara, Utah.*

*Jacob Peart, Jr.,
March 1858. St. George,
Utah. Used by
permission, Utah State
Historical Society, all
rights reserved.*

community of Shunesburg was established in the spring of 1862.[4] Not far above where the East Fork and the North Fork converge, a name and date have been carved into the rock reading, "S. Parker, April The 5, 1869." Samuel Parker was one of the early settlers of Shunesburg.

Brigham Young also sent out an exploring party to the southeast of the Great Salt Lake Valley. In October of 1854 a group under William D. Huntington and Jackson Stewart set out to examine the southeastern part of the territory. Following essentially the reverse of John W. Gunnison's route from the previous year to the Green River, they then turned and crossed the Colorado at present-day Moab. Heading south and east over much the same route followed by John N. Macomb five years later, the exploring party spent several days in the region along the San Juan River. Here they traded with the Navajos and also examined many of the prehistoric Anasazi ruins in the San Juan–Hovenweep area. Before returning to Salt Lake City, where they arrived in December, Huntington, Stewart, and their fellow explorers left three of their wagons and some of their supplies cached in Spanish Valley along what later became known as Pack Creek.

The report given by William Huntington must have been well received by Mormon leaders, for the very next year, 1855, a call was made for a sizable group of men to establish an outpost in Spanish Valley near today's La Sal Mountains, then known to the Americans and Mormons as the Elk Mountains. The subsequent Elk Mountain Mission, as it was known, was put under the leadership of Alfred N. Billings. The group of forty-one men started their journey in May, following the old but reliable route of the Spanish Trail.

Crossing the high plateaus by way of Wasatch Pass, the party descended eastward along what was later named Ivie Creek. Oliver B. Huntington, clerk of the mission, says in his May 27 entry in the official journal of the company, "Camped among cottonwoods. . . . Immediately opposite was a ledge of perpendicular and shelving rocks. Under one shelf and secure from the weather, [I] discovered marks or hieroglyphics, all painted red. . . . After meeting, some of the brethren went up to see the images. . . ."[5] In his diary, William B. Pace said there were "some eight or ten . . ."[6] who did so.

Today, the red prehistoric pictographs can still be seen from the modern highway along Ivie Creek, while a steep scramble up the canyon's side will also reveal the names of three of the "brethren" from the 1855 expedition. All are accompanied by the year

date. One is that of A. N. Billings, president of the Elk Mountain Mission. A second reads, "I. M. Behunin"; I. M. Behunin was commonly known as Martin. The last is a set of initials, "J. S. R." Joseph S. Rawlins (sometimes spelled Rollins) was the wagon master for the company.

The Billings party reached its destination at the present-day site of Moab in June. It followed up Pack Creek and recovered the cache of equipment from the previous year, built a dam and dug ditches to bring water from Mill Creek, and erected a sizable rock fort. For three months the missionaries traded and interacted with the local Utes. In August a small group even traveled south some forty miles beyond the San Juan River and traded with some Navajos. By the latter part of September, however, trouble and conflict with the local Indians led to the permanent abandonment of the mission.

In 1857 recently elected United States President James Buchanan appointed a non-Mormon governor for Utah Territory. In the mistaken belief that the Mormon people would resist the replacement of Brigham Young, the new governor was accompanied by a force of 2,500 troops. Subsequently, in June of 1858, a U.S. military post, Camp Floyd, was built some miles southwest of Salt Lake City.

Early in the spring of 1860 orders came for a portion of the troops at Camp Floyd to remove to Santa Fe, New Mexico. The civilian guide hired to take them there was a Mormon, Daniel W. Jones. Writing some thirty years later, Jones said that after crossing the Green River there was a desert of some fifty-five miles (actually 80 miles) to Grand River (near today's small town of Mack, Colorado). He went on to say that the troops suffered considerably along this stretch and that some of the soldiers left the trail to search for water. Jones then concludes with the significant statement, ". . . one or two never were found; they either perished or fell into the hands of some hostile Indians."[7]

In 1974 a field crew assisting in an archeological survey of the northeastern portion of Arches National Park reported a carved inscription near Freshwater Spring that read, "J. E. D., 1860."[8] This location is some fifteen miles south of the route of travel of the 1860 company of troops guided by Daniel Jones. There is no contemporary or historical record of any other activity in that area at the time. Possibly, then, the initials are those of one of the soldiers who went looking for water. The muster roll of the military company shows no fewer than three different soldiers whose names have

A. N. Billings, 1855. Ivie Creek canyon, Utah.

J. E. D., 1860.
*Arches National
Monument, Utah.*

W. C. Mitchell, 1861.
*Navajo Canyon,
Arizona.*

the initials J. D. There are actually three nearly identical inscriptions in the immediate vicinity, so perhaps this individual stayed for quite some time at this reliable source of drinking water, or he returned to it at least two additional times.

The Southern Indian Mission, which had its beginnings at Santa Clara, Utah, in 1854, was under the leadership of Jacob Hamblin, known variously as the "Mormon Leather-stocking" and the "Apostle to the Indians." Santa Clara was his home for some fifteen years.[9] Carved into a rock slab formerly located along the bank of Santa Clara Creek was the inscription "J. Hamblin, June 15, 1865." It has now been moved and today is displayed at the Jacob Hamblin house in Santa Clara.

This mission labored mainly among the various Paiute bands of southwestern Utah, but according to the Book of Mormon all Native Americans were "Lamanites," one of the so-called Lost Tribes of Israel, and were to be "redeemed" by taking the Gospel to them. Consequently, in the fall of 1858, Hamblin was directed to lead a group of missionaries to the Hopi villages, across the Colorado River to the southeast. Subsequent visits followed in 1859 and 1860. On this latter trip, however, Navajos ambushed and killed one of Hamblin's party, George A.

Smith, Jr., near today's Tonalea, Arizona. Afterward, Brigham Young requested Hamblin to raise a company of twenty men to go back and bring in the body of the unfortunate victim from where it had been hastily buried. This was accomplished in March of 1861.[10]

On the east side of upper Navajo Canyon, in northern Arizona, is a small prehistoric cliff dwelling. In 1954 an archeological survey team found carved into the canyon wall at the back of the ruin an inscription reading, "W. C. Mitchell, 1861." In 1973, just a few feet from this, a second, fainter inscription was discovered. It stated, "W. C. Stewart, Cedar City Ward, 1861." William C. Mitchell and William C. Stewart were both members of Hamblin's 1861 trip.[11]

Upon completion of the recovery mission, Stewart made an oral report that was copied into the Minutes of the Cedar City Ward. In it he describes ". . . finding an old ancient fort of strong . . . proportions [and] of its being supplied with water . . . [which] comes thro [*sic*] the back part, . . . [and] port holes for shooting out of."[12] Though Stewart does not mention carving his name and the date there, all of these features can be found at the Navajo Canyon cliff dwelling.

Butch Cassidy Was Here

Stewart also adds, "It [the cliff dwelling] was a great curiosity to us, but did not think it secure for us, so we moved up into a canon [sic] which was entirely shut in except the entrance. . . ."[13] Neetsin Canyon, which in a general way fits this description, is upstream a mile or so from the Navajo Canyon cliff dwelling. Just a short way up Neetsin Canyon is Inscription House ruin, named for the supposed 1661 inscription found there in 1909. It is now believed that the heavily weathered date is in reality 1861 and was probably cut by members of the Hamblin party. (See also chapter 2.)

Also in 1861 the Territory of Nevada was formed from what had been the western portion of Utah Territory. Therefore, in the next few years Mormon expansion and settlement was directed to the south along Jacob Hamblin's route of travel. In the complex geology of the Colorado Plateau in this region, the north-south trending Hurricane Cliffs form the dividing line between the plateau and canyon country to the east from the lower basin and desert lands to the west. Once up onto the plateau the successive steps of the Vermilion, White, and Pink Cliffs rise one after the other toward the north. From the Virgin River settlements Hamblin's route took him up and over the rim of the plateau and then in a long, curving arc following, in general, the line of the Vermilion Cliffs. This area, lying north and west of the Colorado River and Grand Canyon, was below the politically determined southern boundary of Utah Territory, but it was, and continues to be, dominated by Mormon and Utah influences. It came to be known as the Arizona Strip after 1863, when the Territory of Arizona was created from what had been the western portion of New Mexico Territory.

The so-called Cotton Mission had been called to southwestern Utah in 1861, resulting in the founding of the town of St. George. With the increasing number of settlers, there was no more room to range livestock, so ranchers began turning to the southeast. Favorable expanses of grassland stretched from the Vermilion Cliffs south to the brink of the Grand Canyon. Water sources, as always, were the key points in securing any livestock range.

Therefore, in an orderly progression from west to east, William B. Maxwell of Grafton (some sources say Rockville) claimed ranches at Short Creek early in 1862 and at Moccasin Springs later that same year. The following spring, 1863, James Whitmore of St. George settled at Pipe Spring, and in the spring of 1864 Levi Savage did likewise on Kanab Creek. Finally,

W. C. Stewart, 1861. Navajo Canyon, Arizona.

W. B. Maxwell. House
Rock Valley, Arizona.
Courtesy of Wesley P.
Larsen.

in 1865, Peter Shirts (sometimes spelled
Shurtz) established a small place for himself
at the farthest point east, on the Paria River.
William Bailey Maxwell was not only one of
the first to bring cattle to the Arizona Strip
area, but was also associated with livestock
there for a longer period of time than nearly
anyone else. Though it postdates his arrival
on the Strip by over fifteen years, he did
leave his name inscribed at least at one place
there. Cut into one of the stone blocks at a
rear corner of the House Rock Ranch building on the north side of the present highway
can still be seen the name "W. B. Maxwell."
There is no date, but it was probably inscribed there when he helped build the structure for the Canaan Cooperative Stock
Company in 1877.[14]

Unrest came to southern Utah and the
Arizona Strip beginning in 1865 with the so-
called Black Hawk War. Ute and Paiute
bands resented the taking over of their tradi-
tional lands by the ever-growing number of
Mormon settlers and their livestock. They
were augmented by bands of Navajos who,
after the Kit Carson military campaigns of
1863 and 1864, were forced westward. The
new Mormon herds on the Arizona Strip
were irresistible lures to the relocated natives. With the killing of James Whitmore
and his herder, Robert McIntyre, by a com-

bined Navajo and Paiute raiding party in
January of 1866, the new settlement of
Kanab and the various ranches were aban-
doned in March.

As a result of these events a company of
the Utah Territorial Militia, under the command of Captain James Andrus, was sent
into the field in the late summer. Their orders called for an examination of the country lying on the west side of the Colorado
River from Buckskin Mountain (today's
Kaibab Plateau) to the Green River. Also,
any hostile Indians were to be "chastised"
and any friendly bands "conciliated." In
short, it was to be as much a reconnaissance
as a punitive expedition.

The company left St. George in the middle of August 1866, and traveled to Kanab
by the established route past Maxwell's
ranches and Pipe Spring. East of Kanab the
way was still familiar, by way of present-day
Johnson Canyon to Skutumpah. A few miles
up this canyon an outlier of the eastern wall
juts outward almost to the old trail and
more modern road. Its huge, flat face re-
minds one of a billboard along today's highways and, in fact, it has been used for just
that. In large, black-painted letters can still
be seen "advertisements" such as "John
Allen, Attorney at Law, Kanab," and
"Kanab Auto Garage Co." Scores of other

inscriptions literally cover the rock wall, dating from the late 1800s through the 1900s, as well as many prehistoric petroglyphs.

One of these engravings reads simply, "F. B. W., 1866." Franklin B. Woolley was the adjutant of the Andrus expedition, and as such he was responsible for filing the official report, making a map of the country explored, and drawing up the muster roll of the company members. His subsequent report is an important first description of the rough canyon country sloping eastward from the high plateaus toward the Colorado River, and his map is probably the earliest portrayal of the region based upon actual exploration. In his report Woolley makes the brief observation, ". . . East from Canab [*sic*] we travel to the N.N.W. up Kanyon Ranche Kanyon [today's Johnson Canyon]. . . ."[15]

From Skutumpah the company traversed new territory, unvisited by white men except for perhaps an occasional trapper during the first half of the 1800s. They crossed the rough divide from the northern reaches of Johnson Canyon into the upper valley of the Paria River, and it was through here that one of their number, Elijah Averett, Jr., was killed in the only encounter with Indians. He was shot on August 26 while crossing what is now known as Averett Canyon, a few miles southwest of the present town of Cannonville,

F. B. W., 1866.
Johnson Canyon, Utah.

E. A., 1866.
Special Collections
Dept., Marriott Library,
University of Utah.

Utah. Woolley's report states, "About 10 oclock A.M. of the 27th we recovered and buried the body of Averett. . . ."[16]

Either then or sometime within the next few years, a rounded sandstone slab was placed on the grave with "E. A., 1866" crudely carved into one side. This original stone and inscription can still be seen not far to the north of the present graded dirt road that follows the approximate route of the Andrus expedition between Skutumpah and Cannonville. The more elaborate monument behind it was erected in 1929.

From the upper valley of the Paria River the exploring company skirted the southern end of Table Mountain and descended the headwaters of the Escalante River to Potato Valley around the present-day town of Escalante. Their way to the east and southeast being blocked by the rugged gorges of the Escalante River and its tributaries, Andrus and his men followed Pine Creek northward to the forested slopes of the Aquarius Plateau (Boulder Mountain). From various points along the cliff-lined top the company took in views stretching for many miles in a half-circle from the northwest to the southeast. Mistakenly believing that they could see the junction of the Grand and Green rivers far off to the northeast, which was one of their objectives, the militia turned back westward and headed for home by way of the Awapa Plateau past Grass Valley to the Sevier River. There they reached the road leading south to St. George, where they arrived by mid-September.

Continued efforts by companies of the Utah Territorial Militia gradually broke the resistance of the various Ute and Paiute bands. Black Hawk, after whom the "war" was named, finally made peace with the Mormons the next year. The raiding decreased and an official peace treaty was signed in 1868, after which the southern Utah and Arizona Strip settlements were once again repopulated.

SIX

EXPLORATION OF THE COLORADO RIVER AND ITS TRIBUTARIES

1869–1873

The above heading comes from the title of a historic volume authored by John Wesley Powell and published by the Government Printing Office at Washington, D.C., in 1875. For some 328 years, ever since the first European encounter with the Colorado River in the Grand Canyon by the exploring party of Lopez de Cardenas in 1540, people had wondered and speculated about the course and nature of that stream through the region of the Colorado Plateau. Many had reached the river by overland routes to its relatively few crossing places; parties had followed stretches of its rim, stymied, though, from reaching its shores by the flanking walls of its gorges; and a few individuals had even braved short distances by boat on the waters of the stream itself. But no one had as yet navigated the entire length of the river and its canyons.

In 1868, however, a party led by Major John W. Powell was exploring the White River region in the northwestern part of what was then the Territory of Colorado. A geologist from Illinois Wesleyan and Illinois State Normal Universities, Powell got the idea to descend the canyons of the Colorado River with a scientific party the following year. Access to the river would be by way of its principal tributary, the Green, the Colorado itself being formed by the junction of

that stream and the Grand River in the heart of the Colorado Plateau. It may be recalled that it was not until 1921 that the Grand River was renamed the Colorado, thus politically extending that stream actually into the state of the same name.

Accordingly, Powell and his party, consisting of ten men and four boats, departed the railroad town of Green River, Wyoming, on May 24, 1869. In the next six weeks they made their way down eight major canyons, and when they arrived at the old Spanish Trail crossing a short distance above today's town of Green River, Utah, there were nine men and three boats. One boat had been lost in a rapid and one crew member had left in the Uinta Basin. The exploring party then descended the smooth waters of Labyrinth and Stillwater Canyons before negotiating the rapids of Cataract Canyon, which confined the beginnings of what was then the Colorado itself. Finally, the boats reached the calm stretch that Powell later called Glen Canyon.

Camp, the nights of August 1 and 2, was at the short box canyon not far below the mouth of the San Juan River that the party christened Music Temple. Though none of the diaries or journals mentions the fact, three of the men, Oramel and Seneca Howland (brothers), and William Dunn, cut their

Dunn, 1869. Mount Dellenbaugh, Arizona.

names and the date at Music Temple. This was most likely done on August 2, while Major Powell spent the greater part of the day attempting to climb out of the canyon to take topographic observations.[1] Two years later, in 1871, Frederick Dellenbaugh wrote, "On a smooth space of rock we found carved by themselves the names of Seneca Howland, O. G. Howland, and William Dunn . . . three men of the first party . . . in 1869."[2]

After making their way through Marble Canyon and most of Grand, Major Powell and his men reached a particularly difficult-looking rapid since named Separation. There, for various reasons that have been amply detailed in other accounts, the same three individuals who had left their names in Music Temple now decided to leave the river party, climb out of the canyon, and make their way across the plateau north to the Mormon towns. Powell later learned, through the efforts of Jacob Hamblin, that the trio had been killed by members of the Shivwits band of Paiutes. New information, however, brought to light in 1993, suggests that they may have actually been killed by paranoid Mormons still distrustful of U.S. "government" agents.[3]

Either way, the only trace of the three unfortunate men is a dim inscription left near the summit of Mount Dellenbaugh. Lightly scratched into the surface of a volcanic boulder is the name "Dunn" and the year date, "1869." Underneath that is the word "Water," with an arrow pointing off to the north. Visible in that direction, about six miles distant, is the watercourse of Parashant Wash.[4]

Dunn and the Howland brothers separated from the river expedition on August 28. They followed up what is now called Separation Canyon and climbed out to the plateau above before striking out toward what was later named Mount Dellenbaugh. Researchers who have retraced the trio's route estimate that they probably reached the mountain by August 31. Water by now would have been a critical need, and Dunn probably made his way up the mountain to find out what prospects might be seen from its high elevation. The shortage of time would explain the light scratching of the inscription.

Abandoning one of the boats, Powell and his remaining men finally exited the canyon and reached the mouth of the Virgin River on August 30. For him there was no use in going farther. The river had already been charted up to this point by Joseph C. Ives in 1858. As for exploration, that had ended at the Grand Wash Cliffs. But as soon

as Powell arrived back in the East, he began making plans for a second, more thorough and scientific, examination of the Colorado and its tributaries.

In 1870 Major Powell returned to Utah. Arrangements were made for supplies to be brought to certain selected points along the Green and Colorado Rivers. Understandings were also made with the Paiutes north of the Grand Canyon, so there would be no untoward incidents if encounters were made with the second river expedition. At the conclusion of his summer's work, Powell was invited to participate in a peace conference with the Navajos at Fort Defiance. He therefore returned east by way of northern Arizona and New Mexico.

The party included Powell and two of his associates plus Jacob Hamblin and four other Mormons. Crossing the Colorado at the mouth of the Paria River close to the end of October, the eight men traveled by way of the Hopi mesas and then east toward the fort. They must have stopped, and probably camped, at Tuye Spring, near today's Steamboat, Arizona, trading post. Cut into a large rock near the spring is the name "W. H. Graves, OT 30, 70." Walter H. Graves was a topographer for the Powell surveys and was one of the two men accompanying the Major back east.[5]

At the conclusion of the peace conference on November 5, Hamblin and his four companions started back to Utah. Once again they more than likely camped at the water source of Tuye Spring. The names "N. H. Terry" and "E. J. Potter" are both still to be found incised into the same rock boulder and very near that of Graves. They also both include the same date, "NO 7, 1870." Nathan Terry and Elijah Potter are listed in the writings of Jacob Hamblin as two of the four "brethren" who went with him to Fort Defiance.[6] The Tuye Spring location is also an easy two days' travel west of the fort.

With all arrangements made, and this time with governmental backing, the second Powell expedition was launched in 1871. The May 22 departure was once again from Green River, Wyoming. By the middle of September the party of eleven men and three boats was nearing the junction of the Green and Grand. On September 14, they camped on the west bank of the Green, only some eight miles above the confluence. The next day Powell and three others spent the morning ascending the canyon wall to make topographic observations.

Today, two inscriptions can still be seen from this side excursion. They are carved into a rocky outcropping near the summit of a long, narrow ridge high above the Green

W. H. Graves, OT 30, 70. Near Steamboat, Arizona.

N. H. Terry, E. J. Potter, NO 7, 1870. Near Steamboat, Arizona.

C. E. Ex. 1871.
Canyonlands National
Park, Utah.

W. C. Powell, 1871. Glen
Canyon, Utah.
Special Collections
Dept., Marriott Library,
University of Utah.

F. M. Bishop, 1871.
Glen Canyon, Utah.
Special Collections
Dept., Marriott Library,
University of Utah.

Steward, 71.
Glen Canyon, Utah.
Special Collections
Dept., Marriott Library,
University of Utah.

River. One reads, "C. E. Ex. 1871," while the other is the initials "A. H." The former stands for Colorado Exploring Expedition, an informal name by which the river party was sometimes known. The initials are undoubtedly those of expedition member Andrew Hattan, for in his journal entry for September 15, Stephen V. Jones states, "Soon after breakfast Major [Powell], Jack [John K. Hillers], Andy, and myself started to climb out."[7]

After once again battling the rapids of Cataract Canyon, the Colorado Exploring Expedition, while drifting through the tranquility of Glen Canyon, camped, as did the 1869 expedition, at Music Temple. In his journal entry for October 5, Walter C. Powell, the Major's nephew, wrote, "We placed our names by the side of it [the O. G. Howland, 1869, inscription] and I carved mine . . . and one or 2 others. . . ."[8] Before being flooded by the reservoir waters of Lake Powell, those three inscriptions could be clearly seen, all giving the year date of 1871. They were W. C. Powell, F. (Francis) M. Bishop, and J. (John) F. Steward.

One of the principal differences between this 1871 river expedition and that of 1869 was the time allotted. This second voyage was not going to attempt to go all of the way through the canyons in but one field season. The party stopped at the Colorado River crossing at the mouth of the Paria River on October 23. There the boats were cached and equipment left that was not needed until the next year. The winter's base camp was near the Mormon town of Kanab, where the topographic observations were translated into the preparing of a map of the river. Also started was the triangulation and surveying of the plateau area surrounding Kanab and south to the Grand Canyon.

Butch Cassidy Was Here

Another task undertaken that winter was the exploration for routes to get food rations to the next year's river party. Accordingly, in December, Major Powell, accompanied by three others, left to find a way down to the Colorado by way of Kanab Creek. On New Year's Day, 1872, the party returned, having succeeded in reaching the river. They also brought the information that they had been able to pan gold from the sands of the Colorado. The telegraph operator at Kanab was so impressed with this that it was telegraphed as a news item to Salt Lake City.

This unwittingly precipitated a bona fide "gold rush." For the next four months prospectors and miners poured into the Kanab area, forming a nearly steady flow of men up and down Kanab Canyon to and from the river.[9] In October of 1941, a geological party led by National Park Service naturalist Edwin D. McKee found and photographed, high on the wall of the canyon a few miles up the creek from the Colorado, a deeply carved inscription that read, "A. Starr, A.D. 1872."[10] This was probably placed there by Albert Starr, whose family had settled in Kanab in 1869. That Al Starr was interested in mining prospects is shown by his gold placer claims in Glen Canyon later on in the 1880s.

In the late spring of 1872, before the second leg of the river voyage could begin, one other job had to be taken care of. The previous season one of the three boats had been left at the mouth of the Dirty Devil River in Glen Canyon. An overland party would have to be sent to retrieve it and bring it down the river to the other two at Lee's Ferry. This party, led by Almon H. Thompson, followed the 1866 route of James Andrus to Boulder Mountain (the Aquarius Plateau) and then struck off eastward across the Waterpocket Fold, through the Henry Mountains, and then southeast down to the mouth of the Dirty Devil.

While Thompson and the remainder of the land party retraced their steps back to Kanab, four members of the group readied the cached boat, shoving off onto the river on June 26. That afternoon they camped near a prehistoric pueblo ruin, later referred to as Fort Moqui, a short distance below the mouth of White Canyon. Three of the four, who left written accounts of the trip, all say that they spent the afternoon at the old ruin.[11] One of them left an inscription incised into a stone of the building reading, "J. Powell, 1872, June 27th." Immediately below was the abbreviation "W Ex Ex."

The latter stood for the Western Exploring Expedition, another informal name for the year's river and map-making party.

A. Starr, A.D. 1872. Kanab Canyon, Arizona. Courtesy of Dove Menkes.

J. Powell, 1872, June 27th, W Ex Ex. Glen Canyon, Utah. Special Collections Dept., Marriott Library, University of Utah.

J. Powell, of course, was for John Wesley Powell, the leader of the expedition and survey. Major Powell, however, was not along on the overland trip to the Dirty Devil River, so one of the four boatmen, more than likely Frederick Dellenbaugh, must have been responsible for cutting the name. If the date given is correct, it was done on the morning after they camped, as they departed at 9:00 A.M. on the 27th.[12]

One of Powell's favorite places in all of the Colorado River canyons was Music Temple, a vast chamber carved out of the rock with a clear, deep pool of water at its end, bordered with vegetation. Both his 1869 and 1871 river parties had camped there, and so now did the small group bringing down the cached boat in 1872. In fact, they stayed there for three consecutive nights, waiting out a lingering rainstorm, before finally leaving early in the afternoon of July 11. Earlier, however, three of the four men left their names in Music Temple.

These three inscriptions were "J. K. Hillers, 1872–71," "F. S. Dellenbaugh, 1871–72," and "W. D. Johnson, 72." In his written account, Frederick Dellenbaugh states, ". . . camped at the Music Temple, where I cut Jack's [John K. Hillers's] name and mine under those of the Howlands and Dunn."[13] In William D. Johnson's diary

entry for July 11 he says, "About noon we went up to the [Music] Temple and carved our names in large letters in the rock."[14] The fourth member of the group, James Fennemore, left no known account of the trip, and before the site was flooded by the rising waters behind Glen Canyon Dam, no mention was ever made of his name being in evidence.

The reunited river party left Lee's Ferry on August 17 for the final run through Marble and Grand Canyons. On September 7, however, upon reaching the mouth of Kanab Creek, Powell abruptly decided to terminate the river trip. Concern over high water levels was the reason given. The three boats were abandoned a short distance up Kanab Creek, and the men shouldered what supplies they could before starting the long trek up the canyon and back once again to the town of Kanab.

Most of the members of the Powell survey remained on for the next several weeks mapping the different sections of the region. By November 30, the topographic work was completed and the party was disbanded. Only three of the original members stayed to assist with the preparation of the final map. They continued to utilize Kanab as their base of operations. Several miles north of the town Cave Lakes Canyon comes in from

 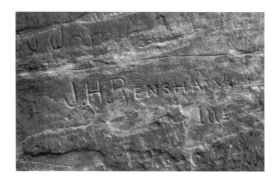

the west. Named for the several rather deep, cave-like alcoves that line its walls, two of them contain large pools of water. These two also have many inscriptions carved into their flanking sides, several of which date from the 1800s.

Two of these inscriptions read, "F. S. Dellenbaugh, C. R. Ex., Buffalo, N.Y., Jan. 25, 1873," and "J. H. Renshaw, Ill.s." Frederick S. Dellenbaugh, referred to earlier, was from Buffalo, New York, and had been a member of Major Powell's river expedition of 1871–72. After the breakup of the survey party he was one of those remaining in Kanab to assist with the map preparation. Even in later years Dellenbaugh referred to the survey as the Colorado River Expedition, the "C. R. Ex." of the inscription. John H. Renshawe, from Lacon, Illinois, did not participate on the river voyages, but joined the survey at Kanab in the latter part of November 1872 to assist with the topographic work.

The misspelling of Renshawe's last name (it is lacking the "e" in the inscription) is probably explained by Dellenbaugh's journal entry for January 26, 1873: "John and I took a ride up to the Cave Lake. . . . Carved our names in the cave."[15] It sounds as if Dellenbaugh may have carved the inscriptions for both of them, and in doing so inadvertently left the final "e" off of Renshawe's name. Less easily explained, however, is why Dellenbaugh's inscription contains the date of the 25th, when his journal entry telling of the carving of the names is for the 26th.

On February 16, the finishing touches were placed on the final version of the map. While Thompson and Renshawe remained at Kanab, Dellenbaugh and Hillers took the now completed result of the survey's long labors north to Salt Lake City. There, on the 26th, it was entrusted to Wells, Fargo & Company for shipment back east to Washington, D. C., and Major Powell.

SEVEN

THE GRAND CANYON REGION

1870–1899

For the some 329 years separating Lopez de Cardenas's reaching the Grand Canyon and Major Powell's first river voyage through the chasm, the region was little visited. The next documented trip actually descended into the gorge, or at least one of its major side canyons. On his way from the lower Colorado eastward to the Hopi pueblos during the summer of 1776, Franciscan padre Francisco Garces was led by his Hualapai guides down to what he called Rio de Jabesua, today's Havasu Creek.

After spending a few days among the Havasupai Indians living there, Garces was led up and out of the canyon before proceeding to the east. He eventually arrived at the brink of the main gorge of the Grand Canyon, evidently in the area of today's Grand Canyon Village on the south rim. Garces bestowed upon it its first documented name, Puerto de Bucareli, in honor of the Viceroy of New Spain. Following his polite, but firm, rebuff from preaching the Gospel to the Hopis, Garces spent one more day and night with the Havasupais in their canyon home before once again wending his way west and south and eventually back to his home mission at Tubac in southern Arizona.

American trappers during the first half of the 1800s no doubt saw the Grand Canyon, but from its lack of streams providing good beaver habitat, they spent little time there. Two parties in the springs of 1827 and 1828, led by Thomas Smith and George Yount respectively, descended the Meriwhit-ica-Spencer Canyon drainage in the western part of the region. However, upon reaching the main Colorado they promptly retraced their steps and left. One author, in a book published in 1961, said that "There are American inscriptions dated in 1828 on the walls of the Grand Canyon of the Colorado River," but unfortunately provided no source for his statement or other details.[1] Mountain man and trapper William S. "Old Bill" Williams reportedly spent several days on the rim of Marble Canyon, in the eastern part of the region, in the late spring or early summer of 1834, but did not attempt to go down into the canyon itself.

As mentioned in chapter 4, Lieutenant Ives and his party reached the bottom of the Grand Canyon at the mouth of Diamond Creek in 1858, and shortly thereafter also descended into Havasu Canyon. In the spring of 1863, Jacob Hamblin and a group of missionaries, on Jacob's sixth trip to the Hopi villages, also visited the Havasupais in their canyon abode. Occasional Mormon deer hunters from the southwestern Utah settlements scouted the forested heights of

the Kaibab Plateau to the north of the canyon in the decade of the 1860s, giving it the name Buckskin Mountain. But it was not until after the first river voyage of Major Powell in 1869 that the Grand Canyon region became much more frequented.

One account says that John C. Naegle, of Toquerville, Utah, ran horses and some cattle on the western slopes of the Kaibab as early as 1865. But if this is true, this endeavor must have been interrupted by the Black Hawk Indian difficulties of 1866–68. Afterwards, however, with the subsequent return of settlers and cattlemen to the Arizona Strip region north of Grand Canyon, the Canaan Cooperative Stock Company was formed. Headquartered at Pipe Spring in 1870, it was placed under the supervision of Anson P. Winsor. Reorganized as the New Canaan Stock Company the following year, the headquarters were moved some twenty miles to the west to Canaan Spring. Pipe Spring, in the meantime, became the central ranch of the Church-owned Winsor Stock Growing Company, which formed in 1873.

All through the 1870s the Mormon cattlemen ranged their livestock from the Hurricane Cliffs on the west to the Kaibab Plateau on the east and as far south as the brink of the Grand Canyon itself. By the second half of the decade they were even run-

ning small herds out southeast onto today's Walhalla Plateau, which they called Greenland. In 1877 the ever-increasing numbers of cattle were finally pushed on across the plateau and east as far as the rim of Marble Canyon. These herds would spend the summer in the higher, forested heights of the Kaibab and winter in the lower, grass-covered expanse of House Rock Valley.

To serve as a headquarters for this new rangeland, the Orderville United Order and the Canaan Stock Company constructed a two-room rock ranch house, which still stands on the north side of the present highway. Carved into the cornerstone at the lower left of the front of the building are two names, "E. R. Adair" and immediately below, "J. G. Bleak." In the 1870s, Elijah R. Adair was the ranch superintendent for the Orderville United Order and James G. Bleak was the secretary-treasurer of the Canaan Stock Company. Though there are no dates accompanying the names, they were more than likely placed there in 1877 when the rock structure was being built.[2]

In 1879 the Winsor Stock Growing Company was merged with the Canaan Stock Company. On March 15 of that year George Mace wrote his name and that date in charcoal on a wall of Slide Canyon, an eastern tributary of Kanab Canyon, draining

E. R. Adair, J. G. Bleak. House Rock Valley, Arizona.

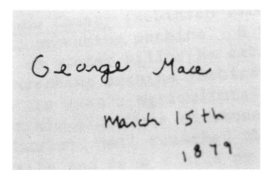

George Mace,
March 15th, 1879.
Slide Canyon, Arizona.
Courtesy of Michael A.
Dussinger.

Lacy Stilson,
Aprl 2, 1882. Snake
Gulch, Arizona.
Courtesy of Michael A.
Dussinger.

off the western slope of the Kaibab Plateau. Mace was a resident of Kanab, Utah, some twenty-five miles to the north, and probably had some cattle in the area.[3]

As already mentioned, the Orderville United Order, a cooperative community in Long Valley north of Kanab, began moving herds of livestock to the Kaibab Plateau and House Rock Valley in 1877. By 1881 it was running some five thousand head of sheep and five hundred cattle. The cooperative also operated several farms in the region to produce alfalfa hay for supplemental winter feed. One of these was in Nail Canyon, the southern head of Snake Gulch.

Deeply carved into the north wall of Snake Gulch is the name "Lacy Stilson, Aprl 2, 1882." Stilson and his family of twelve were members of the Orderville United Order, and he operated only the second threshing machine in the area. In 1882 he went to work on the Denver & Rio Grande Western railroad grade in Emery County, Utah,[4] and probably left his inscription as a record before he left.

While Anson Winsor was at Pipe Spring, a substantial stone-block "fort" was built encompassing the spring for him and his family, and it became known as Winsor Castle. In 1888 it was sold to cattleman Benjamin F. Saunders.[5] Several old names and

dates can still be seen written or carved into the rock walls. "L. Y. Brown, Ren Brown," and "H. A. Brown," probably relatives, all left their names and what appears to be a date of "1888" along the second-story balcony of the "north" structure of the fort. Possibly they were employees of the new owner, and upon their arrival recorded their names.

By 1895, Saunders, a non-Mormon, had completely bought out the Canaan company. Starting in 1893, Preston Nutter, also a Gentile, acquired most of the rangeland in the far western part of the Arizona Strip, between the Grand Wash Cliffs on the west and the Hurricane Cliffs on the east.

The Powell voyages, and especially the subsequent Kanab Canyon gold excitement, opened up the Grand Canyon area to prospecting and mining. It is likely that a number of prospectors, though certainly not many, penetrated the region in the 1860s during the mining boom west of the canyon in southern Nevada. In 1864, James Ferry led a small party of hopeful miners up into the lower end of Grand Canyon for some twenty miles above the Grand Wash Cliffs before retreating back down the river. In later years William H. Hardy told of prospecting in Cataract (today's Havasu) Canyon in the late spring of 1866.

But not many miners were attracted to the difficult and forbidding region until the decade of the 1870s. The sheer size and ruggedness of the terrain, plus the lack of adequate food and sufficient water, greatly restricted the number of prospectors into the canyon itself. No large strikes were ever made, but by the end of the 1890s very probably all of the canyon's alcoves, amphitheaters, and side gorges had been searched for any signs of mineral ore. A few of these wandering prospectors did take the time to stop and leave their names and the date carved or written on a cliff side or rock boulder.

One of the earliest documented prospectors and miners in the region was William B. Ridenour, who spent over thirty years in the western part of the Grand Canyon, south of the Colorado River, in what is today part of the Hualapai Indian Reservation. He

claimed that he and three companions had been driven out by the Indians in 1874,[6] but five years later, if not sooner, he was back again. In a cave on the northwest wall of Meriwhitica Canyon, just a few miles from where it joins Spencer Canyon and the Colorado River, Ridenour and John Tillman, a fellow prospector, incised their names in small, neat letters, "W. B. Ridenour" and "J. Tillman," along with a date of "Dec. 9th, 1879." Ridenour and Tillman remained partners in various mining ventures for at least the next several years.[7]

Many miles to the east, Grapevine Creek descends steeply to the Colorado River from the Grand Canyon's south rim. Just a short distance west of where today's Tonto Trail crosses the creek, under a small cliff overhang, are the words "Hotel de Willow Creek," along with the further notation, "P. D. Berry, R. H. Cameron, April 20, 1890." Willow Creek was an early name for present-day Grapevine, while the title "Hotel" was probably a tongue-in-cheek reference to a camping spot.

Peter D. Berry and Ralph H. Cameron were both well-known prospectors and miners in the eastern part of the Grand Canyon in the 1890s. Berry had first come to the Grand Canyon in 1888, while Cameron had arrived with the new railroad in Flagstaff in

L. Y. Brown,
June 5th, 1888.
Pipe Spring, Arizona.

Ren Brown, 1888;
H. A. Brown, 1888.
Pipe Spring, Arizona.

W. B. Ridenour,
J. Tillman,
Dec. 9th, 1879.
Meriwhitica Canyon,
Arizona. Courtesy of
Dove Menkes.

1883. During an extensive prospecting tour in the spring of 1890 they filed numerous mining claims. Two of these were made April 19 on Horseshoe Mesa, just a couple of miles east of Grapevine (Willow) Creek.[8] The two Horseshoe Mesa mines were a productive source of copper ore until after the turn of the century.

In the Little Colorado River gorge, about a mile upstream from Blue Spring, an inscription is scratched into the canyon wall reading, "B. Beamer, 1891." This was left by Ben Beamer, a prospector who lived near the mouth of the Little Colorado where it joins the main Colorado River. In an 1892 newspaper article he stated, "I got into the canon by the Tanner trail in February 1890. I have lived there ever since. . . ."[9] He intended to homestead, and for a house rebuilt a prehistoric Pueblo ruin under a ledge on the south bank.

Topographic mapping and geologic study on the north side of the Grand Canyon continued through the 1870s and early part of the 1880s as an outgrowth of the two Powell expeditions. In fact, Powell himself was in charge during the majority of this time period. His more scientific river voyage of 1871 and 1872 and congruent map work under the auspices of the Smithsonian Institution were called the Geographic and Topographic Survey of the Colorado River of the West. Despite official name changes to Second Division of the United States Geological and Geographical Survey and U.S. Geological and Geographical Survey of the Rocky Mountain Region, until 1879 it was known simply as the Powell Survey.

In 1879 the Powell, King, Hayden, and Wheeler surveys were consolidated into one entity, the United States Geological Survey. Clarence King was appointed director. At the same time Powell was made the head of the newly created Bureau of American Ethnology. One of King's first acts was to assign the completion of Powell's study of the geologic history of the Grand Canyon region to Clarence E. Dutton. Fieldwork was done during the summer and early fall of 1880.

Sometime during the first half of the 1900s an inscription was found carved into the trunk of a Ponderosa pine at Point

Imperial, on the east rim of the Kaibab over-looking Nankoweap Basin. The carving was first recorded in some field notes of National Park Service naturalist Edwin D. McKee in the 1930s.[10] The inscription read, "U S G Survey, Sept. 3, 1880." Beneath this were two sets of initials, "W. Mc." and "E. A.," and the name "J. J. Pickett."

The first part of the inscription was un-doubtedly left by the geologic party headed by Clarence Dutton. His summer's fieldwork culminated with a pack trip to the Kaibab Plateau, where he reached the rim at what he named Point Sublime, Bright Angel Point, Cape Royal, and Cape Final. In his 1882 monograph, *Tertiary History of the Grand Canon District,* Dutton states, "Leaving Point Final we return northward, keeping now near the eastern front of the Kaibab. . . . North of the Kwagunt is another [large amphitheater], cut out of the East Kaibab monocline, and it opens into the lower por-tion of the Marble Canon."[11] Though Dut-ton does not specifically mention either Point Imperial or Nankoweap Basin, the lat-ter is the unnamed amphitheater he does de-scribe as "north of the Kwagunt." Point Im-perial is the highest point along the entire eastern length of the Kaibab, and would have certainly been visited by Dutton's party.

The initials and name were very likely those of members of the survey group. Un-fortunately, a complete list of the men mak-ing up Dutton's party is not known to exist. The Ponderosa pine itself is no longer to be found at Point Imperial. In July 1966 it was part of a group of trees cut down due to an infestation of bark beetles. However, the portion of the trunk containing the 1880 in-scription was cut out and is now in the Grand Canyon National Park Museum Col-lection at the South Rim.

In 1881, Major Powell replaced Clarence King as the director of the U.S. Geological Survey. Remembering the unusual tilted strata of some of the rock layers lining the Marble Gorge portion of the Grand Canyon during his river expeditions of 1869 and 1872, Powell assigned Charles D. Walcott to work out the geologic stratigraphy of this eastern part of the great chasm. This field-work was carried out during the late fall and winter of 1882–83. The Major himself helped to supervise the construction of what became known as the Nankoweap Trail in November of 1882, so that pack animals, equipment, and supplies could be brought down into this remote corner of the Grand Canyon.

This trail, like many "modern" ones of the canyon, followed a dim Native American pathway into the gorge. From today's Saddle

E. A. Grand Canyon, Arizona. Courtesy of Grand Canyon National Park.

J. J. Pickett. Grand Canyon, Arizona. Courtesy of Grand Canyon National Park.

Mountain, near the eastern rim, it winds precipitously downward into the depths below until it reaches Nankoweap Creek. A few miles up one of the northwest forks of the creek, directly beneath Seiber Point, is the site of the base camp established by the small party while they spent the next few weeks studying the rock strata of the surrounding basin. There is a sheltered, but somewhat open, area and a small spring.

Here, on the side of a large rock boulder, an outline caricature of a man's figure has been incised. Above this is an inscription, "J. HA NO-13, 1882." In his report to Powell the next year, Walcott says, ". . . I was left by you, November 26, at the Trail camp, in Nun-ko-weap [*sic*] Valley. . . . The party consisted of Charles H. Haskell, collector; John Brown, cook; Joseph Hamblin, packer."[12] The "J. HA" is no doubt the abbreviated name of Joseph Hamblin, who was, incidentally, the oldest son of Jacob Hamblin.

Powell remained as head of the U.S. Geological Survey for a dozen more years, and further geologic study of the Grand Canyon region continued on into the 1900s. Coincidentally enough, the man who replaced Powell as director in 1895 was Charles Walcott.

Across the Colorado River, at and beyond the south rim, the influx of prospectors had markedly increased after construction of the Atlantic and Pacific Railroad across northern Arizona in 1882 and 1883. As a result, there was also increased interaction between those prospectors and the only Native American tribe living within the walls of the Grand Canyon, the Havasupai. In the fall of 1884, General George Crook, commander of the military's Department of Arizona, left his headquarters near Prescott for a brief visit to these Indians.

Parts of three days were spent with the Havasupai, and the nights of November 10 and 11 camp was made at a site near the village. In the diary kept by Captain John G. Bourke, part of his entry for November 11 reads, "Before this [supper] was announced, Harmer had painted the names of all our party on a sheltered rock. . . ."[13] Mr. Alexander F. Harmer, of Philadelphia, Pennsylvania, had been invited along as artist for the expedition. Lieutenant Edgar A. Mearns, who also kept a notebook of the journey, said, "Incised on red sandstone (6 X 5 feet) at camp on Cataract [Havasu] Creek, one mile above the Av-Supai Indian settlement, Nov. 11, 1884, by A. F. Harmer of Phila."[14] He then proceeded to list the names of the fifteen members of the expedition that were placed upon the rock.

Butch Cassidy Was Here

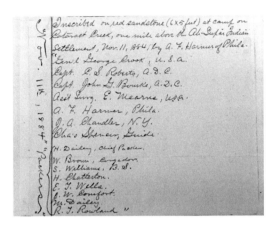

The new railroad and towns, such as Flagstaff and Williams, brought in not only prospectors but a new type of visitor as well. Plain and simple "tourists" began to want to see the spectacle of the Grand Canyon for themselves, and more and more hardy souls were willing to undertake the somewhat rugged trip north from the railroad towns to the south rim. As these numbers steadily increased, some of the prospectors, experiencing but marginal results from their mineral claims, now found it more profitable to cater to the needs of these new visitors.

"Captain" John Hance had first come to the canyon in 1883, and after locating a promising asbestos claim on the north side of the Colorado River, he had improved an old Indian trail leading down what was later called Hance Canyon from the south rim. In 1884 he took his first paying "guests" down this trail, and two years later he had erected his first tent-cabins and even advertised his "Hance Ranch" in the Flagstaff newspaper. Prospector William W. Bass did much the same thing with his "Bass Camp" and Bass Trail farther west near Havasupai Point. Even Ralph Cameron, with his successful copper mines on Horseshoe Mesa, got into the act. In 1890 he took over a water claim at Indian Gardens, a historic Havasupai seasonal camping place halfway down into the canyon, and then greatly improved upon the old Indian trail leading there. The next year Cameron designated this trail as the Bright Angel Toll Road and charged cattlemen, prospectors, and tourists to use it.

What was called the "only first-class hotel at the Grand Canyon" was erected by Cameron's partner, Pete Berry, by 1897. Located near Grandview Point and called the Grandview Hotel, it was a large, rambling, two-story lodge built of native Ponderosa pine logs.[15] Close by was the head of Berry's Grandview Trail, down which tourists could be conducted to the copper mines on Horseshoe Mesa or even farther to the river at the very bottom of the canyon.

Just a few hundred yards from the hotel site and just under the rim, a slight overhang of the limestone rock still protects a list of names written in what was probably wet charcoal. They are "Miss Belle Kerby, Miss Hachett, Brooklyn," and "T. Harris Boughton, Evarts Graham, Rex Mackenzie, Chicago." The date below is "July 12, 1899." From the hometowns listed, as well as the date, these five people were undoubtedly tourist guests at the nearby Grandview Hotel.

Tourism was slower to develop at the

North Rim of the Grand Canyon, primarily because of its greater isolation. Located much farther from any sizable towns, the North Rim region also suffered from its lack of nearby access to a railroad, instrumental in transporting "tourists" in the latter decades of the nineteenth century. In 1908, Grand Canyon was made a national monument, flanked on the north and south by the Kaibab and Coconino National Forests, respectively. National-park status was bestowed in 1919, eliminating cattle and prospecting, but drawing more tourists than ever.

EIGHT

SOUTH-CENTRAL UTAH

1870–1883

The settlement of the south-central part of Utah was directly and indirectly caused by two events. The first was the James Andrus expedition of 1866 (see chapter 5). Heretofore unsettled areas were visited and seen at that time by members of the Mormon militia, and after the cessation of the Black Hawk difficulties at the end of the 1860s, militiamen remembered these regions. The second was a visit to the southwestern Utah settlements, including Kanab, by Brigham Young in the spring of 1870. Kanab had been partially resettled by some of its original pioneers, but after Young's visit he directed a company of families from northern Utah to augment the resettlement.[1]

At the larger of the two "cave lakes" north of Kanab is a carved inscription on the right-hand wall of the deep alcove reading, "H. Kiesel, 1873." Henry Kiesel was one of the early "resettlers" of the town of Kanab.

In the fall of 1870, Brigham Young again visited Kanab. Unlike the first time, however, on this occasion he came in from the north, by way of Upper Kanab (the site of the present town of Alton) and today's Johnson Canyon. Upon seeing these unsettled areas and realizing their potential, he encouraged the townspeople to spread out from their Kanab base. He even went so far as to direct

as many members of the Johnson family as wished to, to take up ranches in what was called Spring Canyon, several miles east of Kanab. This was done the next year.

One of the Johnson brothers, Joel H., wrote in his journal for January 23, 1871, ". . . made arrangements to meet my brothers . . . to look at Spring Canyon ranch. . . . We were highly pleased with the place and . . . therefore we made arrangements for some of us to move there in the spring. . . ."[2] On the cliff side at what has long been known as the Granary Ranch can still be found the deeply cut initials "W. D. J., Jr.," and the date "1871." William Derby Johnson was one of the Johnson brothers and undoubtedly carved this inscription, among the prehistoric petroglyphs, after he and his family arrived in the canyon. Johnson also left his name and the date in Music Temple on the Colorado River when he worked for a time with the second Powell expedition in 1872 (see chapter 6).

Another group of colonists was called by Brigham Young to settle at Kanab in 1871. There then followed a typical trend for many Mormon settlements. The latecomers found that the best tracts of land had already been taken up by the earlier settlers. Some stayed and made-do as well as they could, but others kept on going, to locate

H. Kiesel, 1873.
Near Kanab, Utah.

W. D. J., Jr., 1871.
Johnson Canyon, Utah.

new lands as yet unclaimed. Thus it was that several ranches were established along one of the headwater streams of Johnson Canyon, still known today by its Paiute Indian name of Skutumpah. But on the maps of the period, being made by the Powell survey, the settlement was put down as Clarkston. Just as the Johnson families finally gave their name to what was originally Spring Canyon, several Clark families settled at what was Skutumpah.

Farther east on the Paria River, the "overflow" from Kanab established another small settlement a few miles above Peter Shirts's 1865 ranch claim. Founded in the summer of 1871, it was called by the Paiute name for the stream, Pahreah (note difference from today's spelling).[3] Ten miles or so downstream, just where the Paria River begins to cut an ever-deepening canyon on its way to the Colorado River, many names and dates have been carved into some low, rocky bluffs on the west bank. Due to more recent ones in some cases being placed over earlier ones, and also from the fact that the sandstone here is comparatively soft and easily weathered, the oldest inscriptions are now mostly gone. Between twenty and thirty years ago, however, a local historian and writer recorded the following inscription there that can now no longer be found. It read, "Chris H., July 1873."[4] From the date, this person was possibly a resident of the Pahreah settlement, more than likely checking on cattle in the area.

That spring another settlement was established on the west bank of the Paria River, this time several miles below Shirts's old ranch site. It was named Adairville after one of its founders, Thomas Adair.[5] Another of its early residents was the Goodrich family. Though it is located on private land, and thus difficult to reach today, there is a low burial mound topped by a sandstone slab still to be found at the site of Adairville. Carved on this is the following inscription: "In Memory of Emma, wife of J. H. Goodrich, Born Jan. 11, 1845, Died March 24, 1876."

In 1874 homesteaders spread northward to the upper valley of the Paria River, below the spectacular escarpment of the Pink Cliffs and Paunsagunt Plateau rising to the west. The initial settlement was called Cliff Town, or, more simply, Clifton, and was situated at the junction of the Paria and what was later called Henrieville Creek. After a few years most of the residents moved a few miles farther up both of these streams to more favorable locations. As a result, the towns of Cannonville and Henrieville were founded in 1876 and 1878, respectively.

Hearing favorable reports of what the 1866 Andrus expedition had called Potato Valley, six men from Panguitch, Utah, in the summer of 1875 crossed the plateaus eastward and dropped down into the headwater area of what the Powell survey had named the Escalante River. Here the elevation was lower and the climate milder, so the small group proceeded to spend the next several weeks locating a town site, preparing the land for farming, and digging ditches for water. The following spring saw the arrival of a score of families, and the town was established on the south bank of the river, across from where Pine Creek flowed in from the north. From the river the town was called Escalante.

Like many of the Mormon towns on the Colorado Plateau, Escalante began as a farming community, but quickly acquired its share of ranchers and cattlemen.[6] Stock was ranged from the Upper Valley to the lower elevations of the Escalante Desert, which stretched southeast toward Glen Canyon of the Colorado River. This so-called desert was in actuality covered with a good stand of grass, but the washes, cutting eastward toward the Escalante River from the long escarpment of the Straight Cliffs and Kaiparowits Plateau on the opposite side, were dry the majority of the year. Springs

and associated tanks, then, were key points as sources of vital water.

About thirty-five miles from town is located Red's Well, a developed water source where Coyote Wash begins to cut its canyon. To the northeast, some two miles, the trail drops into the deepening gulch, and not far downstream is an old inscription. Cut into the gray-colored sandstone on the south side, it is very weathered and difficult to see unless the sunlight is at the proper angle. The carving reads, "Arnold, Aug. 1878." It is not known specifically who Arnold was, but in all likelihood he was a resident of nearby Escalante, working cattle in the Red Well–Coyote Gulch area.

To the north of Escalante lies the forest-clad bulk of Boulder Mountain, or the Aquarius Plateau of the Powell survey topographers. It, too, had been crossed by the 1866 Andrus expedition, and the upper valleys of the Fremont River were seen, and remembered, by the militia members. In 1873, Brigham Young sent a group of men to examine the area southeast of the Sevier Valley towns. As a result, the Richfield Cooperative cattle herd was brought into what was called Rabbit Valley in the summer of 1875. Other herds soon followed, and in the next few years several towns were settled in Rabbit Valley.

Arnold, Aug. 1878. Southeast of Escalante, Utah.

A. K. Thurber, 77.
Near Grover, Utah.

J. B. Waters,
March 4, 1880. Capitol
Reef National Park,
Utah.

One of these communities was named Thurber (present-day Bicknell), after the supervisor of the Richfield Cooperative herd, Albert K. Thurber. During the next few seasons, besides attending to his cattle, he was also directed by Church authorities to explore the Fremont River region as much as possible. This he did, as far east as what would later become the town of Hanksville.[7] On these exploratory trips he left his name carved into the rock in at least two places. One is at the base of a triangular-shaped butte in Fish Creek Cove, west of today's Grover, Utah. Here he cut his name, "A. K. Thurber," along with the year date, "77." The other is farther east along Pleasant Creek, where it cuts its way through the upthrust of the Capitol Reef cliffs. Again he incised his initials and last name but this time did not include any date.

As increasing numbers of people came to the Fremont River valley from the more heavily populated regions to the west, settlement progressed steadily eastward. The area around present-day Torrey saw its first settlers in 1878 and nearby Grover in 1880. Unlike most of the towns farther south in what would become Kane and Garfield Counties in southern Utah, Wayne County settlements along the Fremont River west of the Capitol Reef region began with ranchers

bringing in cattle, followed by homesteaders. The first exception to this pattern was what would become known as Fruita, in the heart of today's Capitol Reef National Park.

According to some accounts, the area was first homesteaded by Nels (sometimes spelled Neils) Johnson in 1880,[8] though he may not have been a permanent resident at the time. On a large boulder near the base of the towering cliffs on the north side of the river can be made out the name "J. B. Waters," along with a date of "March 4, 1880." It is not known if he was just passing through at that time, but he was definitely a later resident of the small community. Just a few hundred feet to the east he again carved his name, this time with a year date of "1883."

Located at the junction of Sulphur Creek and the Fremont River, the community was originally called Junction until it received its first post office. The name was then officially changed to Fruita, after the many orchards lining the narrow strips of flat valley floor on either side of the river. The amount of arable land, hemmed in by nearly sheer cliffs on all sides, was necessarily limited, and the area never supported more than a dozen or so families. Newcomers had to either acquire land from established residents or move on elsewhere.

One such family was that of Ephraim K. Hanks. They came to the area in 1881, settling several miles south of Junction (Fruita) on Pleasant Creek.[9] There, just where that stream begins to canyon its way through the cliffs of the Waterpocket Fold, was a small tract of arable land. The Hanks family put in two to three hundred fruit trees, the blossoms of which, in the following spring, gave rise to the name Floral Ranch for the settlement. Never more than a few families ever lived here, and all of them were related to Eph Hanks by either blood or marriage.

Less than a mile east of the ranch site the trail following down Pleasant Creek passes close by a nose of rock projecting outward from the north canyon wall. On this has been incised the outline of a flying bird along with a date of "1881." Below this a name has been carved, but someone has carefully pecked and chiseled over the letters in an attempt to "erase" the name. Enough remains, however, to make out the block letters spelling "Sidney Hanks." Sidney A. Hanks was one of the sons of Eph Hanks, and he evidently left this inscription soon after the family had settled on Pleasant Creek.

Before coming with his family to Pleasant Creek, Ephraim Hanks resided in Burrville, Utah. Following the death of John D.

Lee in the spring of 1877, Hanks was directed by Church leaders to locate at and operate Lee's ferry on the Colorado River.[10] However, upon Brigham Young's death in August, this plan fell through. But Hanks must have at least traveled to northern Arizona to look over the ferry prospects, as his name, "Ephraim," is cut into one of the cornerstones of the House Rock Ranch building, which was constructed in 1877.

On the eastern side of the Waterpocket Fold the character of the Fremont River valley radically changes. Both to the north and south drab mesas of sandstone and shale border the flat valley floor and winding river. Farther east, where the mesas fall away, barren hills of mudstone and clay continue to hem in the stream. But in long, narrow stretches there were areas of arable land, and in the first half of the 1880s several small settlements sprang up along the Fremont, including Aldridge, Caineville, Blue Valley, and Hanksville.

The town of Blue Valley was settled by several families in the spring of 1883, though a few years later the name was changed to Giles. The original name referred to the bluish-gray color of the soil and surrounding hills. Though it is located many miles to the north, along Mussentuchit Wash in the San Rafael Swell, there is an old

inscription that pertains to the settlement of Blue Valley. It is not dated but reads, "A. Mayhew, Pioneer To The Dirty Devil." The family of Austin S. Mayhew was one of those that came to Blue Valley in 1883, and the name Dirty Devil was at that time applied to what was later called the Fremont River.[11]

The easternmost town along the Fremont is Hanksville. Here, where Muddy Creek comes in from the north, the stream makes a rather abrupt bend to the south and becomes known as the Dirty Devil River. This name had been bestowed by the first Powell expedition in 1869 when they passed by its mouth where it flowed into the Colorado. That name was then extended upstream to its far source in Fish Lake. By the late 1870s, however, when the geography of the region became better known, the Powell survey gave the generally east-west trending part of the stream drainage above Muddy Creek the name Fremont, in honor of John C. Fremont (see chapter 4).

Hanksville itself was named for Ebenezer Hanks, a cousin of Ephraim Hanks of Floral Ranch on Pleasant Creek. The settlement was originally known simply as Graves Valley, said to have been named for Walter H. Graves of the Powell survey, who helped to map the valley and surrounding region in

the 1870s and who left his name inscribed at Tuye Spring in northern Arizona (see chapter 6). The area was settled by Eb Hanks and various relatives in the spring of 1882. Interestingly, Hanks learned of the valley in 1881 from Albert K. Thurber, who had left his name inscribed not too many miles to the west along the canyon of Pleasant Creek.

Charles H. Goold (sometimes spelled Goald or Gould) was a son-in-law of Eb Hanks. He and his family lived in Hanksville for seventeen years, farming and running a few head of livestock. To bring in actual hard cash, Charles spent some winters working at mining camps on the Colorado River.[12] It was undoubtedly on one such occasion that he scratched his name, "C. Goold," and the date, "Jan. 16th, 1897," on a wall of the prehistoric Anasazi ruin known as Fort Moqui, a few miles below the mouth of the Dirty Devil River in Glen Canyon. This was on the east bank of the Colorado, directly across the river from the mining camp of Hite.

North of the Fremont River, far across the intervening hills and desert in what is now Emery County, lies Castle Valley. Down its length ran the old Spanish Trail, and the valley had been traversed many times by Mexican caravans, wandering American trappers, and the government surveying ex-

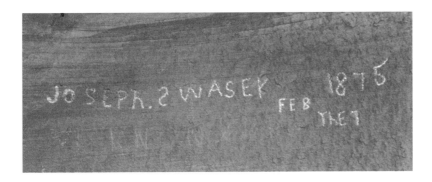

peditions of John W. Gunnison and John C. Fremont (see chapter 4). For decades it was principally a route for getting to and from someplace else, but in the second half of the 1870s that began to change. By 1875 ranchers from the western ranges started to bring their cattle eastward to the Wasatch Plateau and Castle Valley. The higher elevations of the plateau were utilized in the summer, while Castle Valley, and the San Rafael Swell beyond, served as winter ranges.

Among the first of these cattlemen were the Swasey brothers from Juab County. The first record of their bringing their family's cattle to Castle Valley was in 1875.[13] On the canyon wall of the North Fork of Coal Wash, across from what is still locally known as Stinking Spring, the younger of the brothers left this inscription pecked into the rock: "Joseph Swasey, Feb. The 7, 1875." Located in the depths of the San

Rafael Swell, this spot was no doubt a winter camp of the brothers, which would indicate they had been in the region the previous year, 1874. In later years Joe Swasey referred to the flat rock ledge and slightly overhanging canyon wall here as the "Biltmore," insisting that he "slept better here than at the Biltmore Hotel in Kansas City."[14]

Soon after the transient cattlemen came the permanent settlers and homesteaders. Some of these were families of the original stockmen. In 1877 the Church of Jesus Christ of Latter-day Saints directed that a colonizing effort be made in Castle Valley, and by 1881 no fewer than eight settlements had been established on the various creeks and streams flowing eastward across the valley from the high plateaus. Most, such as Emery, Ferron, Castle Dale, and Huntington, remain thriving towns today.

Joseph Swasey, Feb. The 7, 1875. San Rafael Swell, Utah.

NINE

TO THE LITTLE COLORADO

1871–1899

The Little Colorado River in northern Arizona flows in a generally northwest direction from the White Mountains to the Grand Canyon. While the upper portion of the drainage is green and well watered, the lower half cuts through desert and plateau land. Thus, parts of what by the early 1800s the Spanish had named the Rio Colorado Chiquito contained good land ripe for settlement as well as large areas only marginally fit for habitation. Leaders of the Church of Jesus Christ of Latter-day Saints, always on the lookout for future settlement sites, had long had their eye on the Little Colorado River region.

Between 1858 and 1871, Jacob Hamblin and other Mormon missionaries had made close to a dozen trips from Utah Territory to the Hopi villages and were therefore somewhat familiar with at least the lower stretches of the Little Colorado. With the Mormon return to the southern Utah settlements in 1870 and the Fort Defiance treaty with the Navajos later that same year, it was now hoped that the way was clear for expansion across the Colorado and into northern Arizona. But before any attempt at colonization was made, one important obstacle had to be overcome: the crossing of the river. On many of his trips Hamblin had crossed at what the Mormons referred to as the Ute Ford, the same as the El Vado de los Padres, or Crossing of the Fa-

thers, of the Spanish. But this was strictly a pack route completely unsuitable for settlers and their accompanying wagons. He had also crossed a time or two at the mouth of the Paria River, though this was not a ford and required a boat or raft.

The Paria crossing, however, was accessible on both sides for wagons; and therefore it was decided that this would be the entrance point for the Mormon settlement of the Little Colorado River region. In 1871, John D. Lee was directed to settle on the west bank of the Colorado River at what was already known as Lonely Dell. Traveling from his home at the small settlement of Skutumpah, across the Kaibab Plateau and House Rock Valley and up to the Paria from the southwest, Lee and various members of his extended family arrived on, or near, Christmas Day 1871. There is a gap in the diary that was kept by Lee, from December 3 until the 26th, but his entry for this latter date indicates a recent arrival.[1]

At House Rock Spring, west of the river, is a small, neatly lettered inscription that reads, "J. D. Lee, Dec. 25, 1871." At the rate at which the Lee contingent was traveling, this was approximately a three-day trip from their ultimate destination. So there is the probability that the name and date were inscribed at some later time. It is known that

Lee spent two days at House Rock Spring the following April,[2] and he may have cut the inscription then but dated it to commemorate his visit to the site about Christmastime the preceding year.

House Rock Spring and the valley stretching below had received their name from an old inscription located nearby. For nearly a month in the late fall and early winter of 1871, several members of the second Powell expedition (see chapter 6) camped here. One of them, Frederick S. Dellenbaugh, later wrote, "About sunset [of November 8] we passed two large boulders which had fallen together, forming a rude shelter, under which . . . some one . . . had slept, and they had jocosely printed above [on the vertical cliffside] with charcoal the words 'Rock House Hotel.' Afterwards this had served as identification, and Jacob [Hamblin] and the others [Mormons] had spoken of 'House Rock' Spring and House Rock Valley."[3] The two leaning rock slabs are still there, as are the faded remnants of the original printed black letters.

By the fall of 1872, after John D. Lee and his family were firmly settled at Lonely Dell, a ferry boat capable of transporting families and their wagons was directed to be built at the crossing. Also that fall, Jacob Hamblin, on his return from his latest journey to the Hopis, came by way of Moencopi, a small, seasonal farming village of the Oraibi pueblo. Traveling from there northward along the base of the Echo Cliffs and Kaibito Plateau, he, in effect, was scouting the way for the coming wagon road. The ferry was completed in January 1873, with Lee as its operator and beneficiary of any revenue collected. In the coming years, and even until the present time, the location would be known as Lee's Ferry.

Soon after its completion, the ferry was first used by the so-called Arizona Exploring Company in February and again in March. Under the leadership of Lorenzo W. Roundy, the group traveled south and southeast to explore and examine the Little Colorado valley first-hand, then report back to Church authorities.[4] At House Rock Spring is carved the name "L. W. Roundy, Konnoro 18." Roundy is known to have passed by way of the spring on at least two trips to and from Lee's Ferry, in 1873[5] and again in 1876.[6] More than likely this inscription, which has no full date accompanying it, was left during the spring 1873 exploring expedition. The word "Konnoro" is Roundy's misspelling of his hometown of Kannarah, present-day Kannarahville, Utah.

In March 1873, immediately upon the return of the Roundy party, some 250 men and

L. W. Roundy, Konnoro 18. House Rock Spring, Arizona.

S. R. Parkinson,
*May 12, 1873. House
Rock Spring, Arizona.*

Wm. H. Solomon,
*May 12th, 1873. House
Rock Spring, Arizona.*

women were directed to settle the Little Colorado valley. Under the leadership of Horton D. Haight, the so-called Arizona Mission was divided into companies that left the Mormon settlements every few days beginning in April. This was to prevent overcrowding at the various watering places and grazing areas along the route. The "road" followed these key points from place to place, which included House Rock Spring, Jacob's Pools, Soap Creek west of Lee's Ferry, and Navajo Spring, Cottonwood Tanks, and Willow Springs east of the Colorado River crossing. Oftentimes emigrants would rest up to several days at these spots, allowing their livestock and themselves to recuperate from the arduous trip. Because of such extended stays, these areas were prime locations for travelers' names and sometimes the date to be inscribed on the surrounding rocks.

The various companies crossed the Colorado at Lee's Ferry in late April and through May, arriving along the Little Colorado by the first of June. Two of the scores of inscriptions to be found at House Rock Spring are dated "May 12, 1873," one left by "S. R. Parkinson" and the other by "Wm. H. Solomon." According to a journal kept by John H. Standifird, they were part of a company led by Henry Day, and they remained at House Rock from May 10 to May 19. In his

entry for May 11, Standifird stated, "Prayer by Bro[ther] Parkinson,"[7] and for the 18th said, "Bro. William H. Solomon and myself joined together to mess [eat] and travel. . . ."[8]

Across the river and farther south, at Willow Springs, "M. F. Adams, H. K. Perkins," and "Nelson T. Fenton," of an earlier company, all left their names with a date of "May 18, 1873." On May 20, 1873, "B. Y. Perkins" carved his name on one of the many boulders scattered along the base of the first step of the Echo Cliffs. A short distance away, partway up the little gully leading to the spring site itself, is a rather lengthy inscription carved in square-cut block letters. Attributed to the above-mentioned Brigham Y. Perkins, it reads, "Oh That Men Would Praise The Lord For His Goodness And For His Wonderous Works."

Upon reaching the Little Colorado the colonists found the region, notwithstanding the earlier Roundy report, entirely unfit, in their opinion, for settlement. There was also a previously unknown threat from roving Apache Indian bands. For one of the few instances in Mormon colonization, the prospective settlers turned around and started back for Utah Territory. Though it is no longer to be found today, a record of this return was left near Moencopi Wash. In his journal entry for June 13, John H. Standifird

M. F. Adams. Near Willow Springs, Arizona.

H. K. Perkins, May 18th, 1873. Willow Springs, Arizona.

B. Y. Perkins, May 20, 1873, Jan. 9, 1878. Willow Springs, Arizona.

C. C. Allen, June 2, 1873. House Rock Spring, Arizona.

Robt. H. Bradshaw, R. T. Burton, June 2nd, 1873. House Rock Spring, Arizona.

Richd. P. Bradshaw, June 6th, 73. House Rock Spring, Arizona.

said, "Some of the boys wrote on a rock and set it up at a conspicuous place at the spring. 'Arizona Mission Dead—1873.'"[9]

As the first of the returning wagons made their way back along the Echo Cliffs and on across the Colorado River westward, they encountered families still on their way to the Little Colorado from Utah. This was the case at House Rock Spring, where several inscriptions, dated June 2, 5, and 6, can still be seen,

left by C. C. Allen, Richard P. Bradshaw, R. T. Burton, Jr., C. Layton, and Robert H. Bradshaw. One, carved on the wall a short distance to the left of the spring by "Joseph Adams From Kaysville," is more informative. It continues on to state, "To Arzonia [*sic*] And Busted On June 6, A.D. 1873."

After the failure of the Arizona Mission, Brigham Young immediately began preparing the way for a new attempt. First, a new,

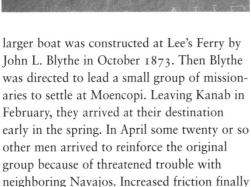

larger boat was constructed at Lee's Ferry by John L. Blythe in October 1873. Then Blythe was directed to lead a small group of missionaries to settle at Moencopi. Leaving Kanab in February, they arrived at their destination early in the spring. In April some twenty or so other men arrived to reinforce the original group because of threatened trouble with neighboring Navajos. Increased friction finally caused the Blythe group to leave Moencopi and return to Utah in May 1874.

One of the reinforcement party left his name, "D. V. Bennett," but with no date, carved at House Rock Spring. At Lee's Ferry on May 9, "All of the brethren and missionaries but Blythe, myself, and Bennett continued on their journey . . ." according to the journal kept by the clerk of the mission, William H. Solomon.[10] "Bennett" was David V. Bennett, a resident of the settlement of Skutumpah, northeast of Kanab. The inscription was most likely done on or about Sunday, May 17, as according to the Solomon journal the trio camped there the nights of the 16th and 17th.[11]

After a meeting between Jacob Hamblin and various Navajo headmen late in 1874, the following fall Brigham Young sent a group of men under James S. Brown, fluent in the Navajo language, to re-establish the Indian mission at Moencopi. This would, hopefully,

further pave the way for another attempt at Mormon settlement of the Little Colorado region the next year. In the spring of 1876 the major colonization effort began with some two hundred men, women, and children. There was no formal gathering, and groups of about ten families each traveled together from Kanab, reporting to their designated leader once they reached the Little Colorado. The leading groups reached their destination by the end of March, but migration continued for many weeks thereafter.

Among the more intriguing inscriptions of the many to be found at House Rock Spring are carvings of the outline of what appears to be four fish, done in the simple, somewhat stylized form of the ancient symbol for Christianity. Now very faint and weathered, and partially covered by growths of lichen, they were recorded by a historical society group making an inventory of the House Rock Spring inscriptions in the latter part of April 1992.[12] To the lower right of the four "fish" was an equally obscure date, which they interpreted as "Nov. 1776." Taking the idea of the fish being Christian symbols, and the date of 1776, the group thought that this was possibly an inscription left by the Catholic fathers Dominguez and Escalante, who passed near here on their epic trek that year (see chapter 2).

However, there are two important reasons to reject this idea. First, according to the official diary of the journey kept by Father Escalante, while the party did pass close by the area of the spring, they did not camp there, and the date was October 24.[13] Secondly, a close and careful examination of the year date carved on the rock wall to the right of the spring reveals it to actually be 1876, not 1776. The Mormon migration to the Little Colorado region that continued through much of that year was, in fact, divided into four companies under four separate leaders.[14] Therefore, a more likely possibility is that the four fish symbols represent each of the Church-initiated colonizing groups of 1876.

At least thirty of the names on the rocks surrounding House Rock Spring date from the 1876 migration. One is that of "D. E. Adams," with "Caroline Adams," dated "Mar. 17, 1876." David E. Adams and his wife were from Alpine County, Utah, Mr. Adams being the "captain," or leader, of his group of ten families. Writing several years after the fact, he described House Rock Spring as "A beautiful place there, plenty of water and grass . . . a crevice from the back or east part from which spurted out water three or four feet in a nice level garden spot, on the south of which had our names carved, wife and I, which is still there. . . ."[15]

Surprisingly, there being so many inscriptions at House Rock Spring dating from the 1876 migration, there is but one such dated example at any of the other watering/camping spots on the east side of the Colorado River. There are none at all at Navajo Spring or Tanner Well and only a single one at Willow Springs. It is that of "E. L. Westover" and is dated "Mar. 27, 1876."

The next four years saw additional colonizing and new emigrants. In 1877 and 1878 settlement was along the major tributary of the Little Colorado, Silver Creek, while the final phase in 1879 and 1880 was along the upper part of the river. Many of the names left at the various inscription locations with these year dates no doubt reflect this continued settlement pattern, though some were also left by already established residents journeying back to Utah for one reason or another.

One such reason was for young couples to travel to the Latter-day Saint temple in St. George, which was completed in 1877. Many newlyweds from the scattered Arizona Territory settlements came to the only Mormon temple in the West for "endowments." Separate from the civil marriage ceremony, the endowment was a religious rite that "sealed" faithful Mormons together for "all eternity." This might be done even months later, when

D. E. Adams, Caroline Adams, Mar. 17, 1876. House Rock Spring, Arizona.

E. L. Westover, 1876. Willow Springs, Arizona.

George M. Haws,
Josephine Haws,
Dec. 13, 1877. Willow
Springs, Arizona.

Geo. Brown Of Summit
Co. UT. To St. Johns,
Sept. 29, 84. Navajo
Spring, Arizona.

time and circumstances allowed. From 1878 until the early 1890s, enough young couples made this journey that the route became known as the Honeymoon Trail.

Carved into one of the rocks at Willow Springs are the names of "George M. Haws" and "Josephine Haws," dated "Dec. 13. 1877." They had been married at the little settlement of Johnson, Utah, east of Kanab, while on the way with their families to the new community of Snowflake, Arizona. This was one of the recently settled Mormon colonies on Silver Creek of the Little Colorado River. They had camped at Willow Springs on their journey south. Some eight months later, on August 5, 1878, George Haws recorded in his journal, "We concluded to go back to St. George [and go] through the temple."[16] In other words, to "go through" the endowment sealing.

By 1877 several families had located at Moencopi as a part of the Indian mission there. In September 1878, Apostle Erastus Snow visited northern Arizona and at that time laid out a townsite at Musha Spring, about two miles north of Moencopi, for a permanent Mormon settlement. It was called Tuba City after Tuvi, Hopi headman at Oraibi and also of the seasonal village at Moencopi. Following establishment of the Mormon town, a permanent Hopi pueblo at Moencopi was also begun.

Even after the initial colonization of the Little Colorado settlements newcomers continued to come and go, some staying, others not. Navajo Spring, several miles from Lee's Ferry on the eastern side of the Colorado, often was the first watering/camping site for travelers after the river crossing. On many of the rock boulders scattered near the base of the Echo Cliffs, names and dates have been painted and carved, many from the late 1800s. One of these is representative of the continued movement to northern Arizona from Utah. The informative inscription reads, "To St. Johns, Geo. Brown Of Summit Co. UT. Sept. 29, '84." However, at Willow Springs, a two- or three-days' wagon journey south, is an equally informative inscription illustrative of the other possibility awaiting prospective settlers. It states, "C. M. Emmon From Kanosh For Orisonia [*sic*] And Busted, April 22, 1883."

The wagon road connecting the southern Utah and the northern Arizona settlements remained in use for many years. In fact, the present-day highways in many cases are simply paved-over portions of the old Mormon route. The crossing of the Colorado River at Lee's Ferry remained in use until the opening of the Navajo Bridge, several miles to the south across the Marble Canyon gorge, in 1929.

TEN

THE FOUR CORNERS REGION

1873–1897

The Four Corners is the designation given to that region of the Colorado Plateau surrounding the point at which the states of Utah, Colorado, New Mexico, and Arizona all touch. The Spanish, as usual, were the first Europeans to enter this area. The winter route of the Spanish Trail was not too many miles to the northeast, while the oft-traveled trail to the Hopis was not very far to the south. American trappers following down the upper San Juan River would have passed but a few hundred feet from the later established point of the Four Corners itself. In the late 1830s and through much of the decade of the 1840s, Mexican raiding parties made their way through the San Juan valley and past the Four Corners, and United States military expeditions threaded their way across the region in the 1850s and 1860s (see chapter 4).

However, it was not until the coming of American prospectors that the first historic inscriptions were recorded. Late in 1860 a large company of miners led by a Captain Charles Baker left the new mining districts of eastern Colorado, arriving in the San Juan Mountains in the southwest part of the territory in March 1861. Finding no promising gold prospects, the company split into three groups to make their way back to civilization. One, led by John C. Turner, headed

southwest toward Arizona.[1] Though no description of their journey was left, geography would dictate a probable route from the mountains down the drainage of the Mancos River to the San Juan and thence across the Navajo country to the southwestern Arizona settlements.

One of the tributaries of the Mancos, cutting northward into the Mesa Verde, is Soda Canyon. Just a short distance up this side gorge and on the eastern side is a prehistoric Anasazi cliff dwelling known as Bone Awl House. Cut into the canyon wall to the left of the ruin site is an inscription reading, "T. Stangl, 1861." Perhaps this is a record of the Turner party of prospectors that had left the Animas River area of the San Juan Mountains and were headed to Arizona.

By the mid-1860s several mining camps had sprung up along the Verde River in north-central Arizona, and in 1866 a party of prospectors under a Colonel Nash came up from Arizona toward southwestern Colorado. They crossed the San Juan River near the mouth of McElmo Creek and followed that stream around the Sierra El Late (today's Sleeping Ute Mountain) and on to the Dolores River. There they divided, one group traveling upstream and eventually to the Colorado settlements on the eastern side

*T. Stangl, 1861. Ute
Mountain Tribal Park,
Colorado.*

*Louis Clift, 1870.
Navajo Spring, Utah.*

of the mountains. The other, however, followed the trace of the old Spanish Trail northwest to the La Sal Mountains and Grand (Colorado) River.

In the fall of 1869 a large group of prospectors left the mining camp of Prescott, Arizona, for the San Juan Mountains, traveling by way of Fort Wingate in northwestern New Mexico. From there a smaller party of eight went on to the San Juan River, and when one of the men recognized the Mancos River coming in from the northeast, they followed that stream up into the mountains. Significantly, the man who recognized the Mancos was Adnah (sometimes referred to as Abner) French, a member of the Baker expedition to the San Juans in 1860–61.[2] This lends further credence to the probability that the Turner group of 1861 did, in fact, descend the Mancos River on their way to Arizona that year, and that the "T. Stangl, 1861" inscription just a short distance up Soda Canyon is from that journey.

At Navajo Spring along Comb Wash, a little over three miles north of the San Juan River, an old inscription is carved into a rock boulder. It reads simply, "Louis Clift, 1870." Situated at the foot of the nearly sheer escarpment forming the western side of Comb Ridge in southeastern Utah, the spring is located near where an ancient In-

dian trail crossed this some twenty-five-mile-long barrier. To the north it gradually merges with the broader Elk Ridge, a southerly extension of the Abajo Mountains. A geologist who did much fieldwork in the Colorado Plateau region in the early 1900s wrote, "There are reports of prospectors . . . east of the Colorado River about Elk Ridge and the Abajo Mountains as early as 1870."[3]

On July 17, 1873, John D. Lee, of Lee's Ferry on the Colorado River, described in his diary a meeting with John Moss, an "old mountaineer," and four companions, on their way to "the San Juan country." Significantly, though, Lee also adds, "He [Moss] . . . reports a splendid country . . ." and continues on with a multi-line description quoting Moss.[4] It is obvious from this that Moss had been to the San Juan region before, probably the previous year.

Specifically, Moss and his party were heading to the La Plata Mountains in southwestern Colorado. La Plata is Spanish for "the silver," and they were so named by the Rivera expedition of 1765. Moss, too, was prospecting for silver and/or gold. Upon crossing the San Juan River just a few miles from Four Corners, the most direct route to the mountains, as earlier prospecting parties had already discovered, was northeast up

the canyon of the Mancos River. Near the upper end of this canyon, on the north side, is a prehistoric Anasazi ruin called Sandal House. A dim date, "5/11/72," is written on one wall. There is no record of any other activity in the area at that time, so this may be a record of Moss's 1872 visit to the region.

Another inscription at Sandal House may very well have been left by other San Juan prospectors. It is the initials "L. A." with a date of "July 8, 1874." At his ferry crossing between the summer of 1873 and the summer of 1874, John D. Lee recorded in his diary no fewer than a dozen different parties on their way to the San Juan country.[5]

One of the four government-sponsored surveys of the 1870s was the United States Geological and Geographical Survey of the Territories, commonly known as the Hayden Survey after its director, Ferdinand V. Hayden. With the mining boom in the San Juan Mountains of southwestern Colorado, the photographic detachment of the survey, under the leadership of William H. Jackson, was working there in 1874. Upon hearing of "ancient towns and ruins" from Moss's men on the La Plata, he was assigned the task of traveling to the Mancos and San Juan to investigate the reports.

Jackson's party, guided by John Moss, left for the Mancos the first part of Septem-

ber. On the evening of the 9th and morning of the 10th, Jackson and some of the others climbed up to what is now known as Two-Story House.[6] Though he does not mention the fact in his diary, Jackson and two of his companions evidently left their names on an inside wall of the ruin. The following year another member of the Hayden Survey, William H. Holmes, also scaled the steep slope of Mancos Canyon up to Two-Story House. In his official report he states, ". . . the plastering of the interior is almost untouched, that with the exception of three names scratched in the soft, thick coat of adobe by Mr. Jackson's party."[7]

Following his work with the Hayden Survey, William Jackson became a well-known photographer in Denver, Colorado. Several years later he returned to Mancos Canyon with several companions to show them the ruins and revisit them himself.[8] Though his 1874 signature in Two-Story House can no longer be seen today, on this later trip he and his party wrote their names in what appears to be pencil lead, on a rock slab lying in the upper level of Sixteen Window House. Located little more than a mile down the canyon from Two-Story House, the inscription reads, "W. H. Jackson, Feb. 23, 87."

In the summer of 1875, Jackson was

L. A., July 8, 1874. Ute Mountain Tribal Park, Colorado.

W. H. Jackson, Feb. 23, 87. Ute Mountain Tribal Park, Colorado.

E. A. Barber. Near Bluff, Utah.

F. Fisher, 1878. Near La Sal Junction, Utah.

once again sent by Hayden to photograph and study more reported prehistoric ruins in the Four Corners region, with his ultimate destination being the Hopi pueblos. As they had the previous year, the party started out from the mining camps of the Animas River in the San Juan Mountains, but this time followed McElmo Wash to the San Juan River, examining the ruins of the Hovenweep area along the way. Turning west, they followed the cliff-lined San Juan valley until it began to cut into a rugged canyon several miles downstream from the present town of Bluff, Utah. In traveling thus, they made one of their camps near a large cliff dwelling on the south side of the river.

Jackson's group gave this ruin the euphonious name Casa del Eco, Spanish for "house of the echo," though today it bears the more prosaic title Seventeen Room Ruin. Scratched into the wall of the deep alcove sheltering the site, just behind the row of rooms, is the name "E. A. Barber." It is not dated, but was undoubtedly left there on August 4, 1875, when the Jackson party visited the ruin.[9] Edwin A. Barber was a newspaper correspondent attached to the Hayden Survey that season for publicity purposes.

The guide for Jackson's party that year was Harry Lee, one of Moss's group of miners on the La Plata River. After their visit to

the Hopi pueblos, Jackson and his men returned to the San Juan River, crossing that stream and working their way northward to the Blue, or Abajo, Mountains in southeastern Utah. From there they finally headed back to Moss's camp at the foot of the La Plata Mountains, where they arrived the first week of September.

The mining prospects of the Abajos must have seemed promising to Harry Lee, as not long afterwards he, John Moss, and another man returned to the "Blue" Mountains.[10] The headwaters of Montezuma Creek drain a short distance eastward and then south from these mountains, and about halfway down Montezuma Canyon to where it empties into the San Juan River, is an inscription. Deeply carved into the rock on the west canyon wall is "H. W. Lee, F '75." Knowing that Harry Lee was, in fact, in the Abajo Mountains in 1875, and knowing that he had returned with the Jackson party in early September, Lee very probably left this record on his later prospecting trip. The capital letter "F" in the inscription likely stands for "Fall."

Undoubtedly influenced by favorable reports from the San Juan miners and the Hayden surveys, cattlemen and settlers began coming into the Mancos and Montezuma valleys of southwestern Colorado by

1877. But these areas were relatively small, and the rapid influx of livestock quickly filled the available ranges. So in 1878, Pat and Mike O'Donnel took their herds northwest into Utah for summer grazing in the comparatively flat, plains-like region stretching to the foot of the Abajo Mountains.[11] Perhaps the inscription "F. Fisher, 1878," carved inside of a small cave in the northern reaches of Dry Valley, was connected in some way with the O'Donnel operation.

However, the grasslands of what would become San Juan County, Utah, were not to remain unused for long. In quick succession after the O'Donnel brothers came three other cattlemen with large herds. The first was Joshua B. "Spud" Hudson in 1879, who came from southern Colorado with some two thousand head of cattle, and early in 1880 a second man by the name of Peters came in with another two thousand head. Later the same year the Lacey Cattle Company brought a large herd from New Mexico.

Known more simply as the L C Company, this latter outfit had its summer ranges on the southeastern and southern slopes of the Abajo Mountains, while in the winter the cattle were moved down into the lower canyons draining south to the San Juan River.[12] In a cave site in upper Butler Wash, one of these northern tributaries, someone carved his initials, "A. E. S." Immediately below are the smaller letters "L C," with no periods. Undated, their presence perhaps signifies a rider for the Lacey Company.

But the largest cattle operation in the region to the northwest of the Four Corners was that of the Carlisles. Though officially named the Kansas and New Mexico Land and Cattle Company because of holdings in those two states, it was known in southeastern Utah simply as the Carlisle Company after its owners, Harold and Edmund S. Carlisle. In May 1883 they bought out the interests of Hudson, Peters, and some smaller outfits, and by the next year were reported to have had over ten thousand head ready for market. The Carlisles controlled the range north of the L C Company, the northern and northeastern flanks of the Abajos serving as summer range and the lower elevations of Dry Valley during the winter season.

Somewhat ironically, in the same cave on Butler Wash that contains the possible "L C" inscription, there is also a rather weathered one done in charcoal on a fallen rock boulder. It appears to be the name "L. Gordon," with a date of "1896." William E. "Latigo" Gordon was the son of Mrs. Harold Carlisle by an earlier marriage. From 1887 until 1897 he was the range foreman for the Carlisle Cattle Company.[13]

A. E. S., L C.
Butler Wash, Utah.

L. Gordon, 1896.
Butler Wash, Utah.

By the beginning of the 1890s, the San Juan County range was overstocked and overgrazed. Cattle prices dropped over all of the West, and the Colorado Plateau region in particular suffered through a lengthy period of drought from 1892 until 1898. The L C Company sold off its interests by the mid-1890s, and the Carlisle Company ridded itself of its cattle operation by 1897, though they continued for several more years with sheep. After 1897 most of the cattle operations in the Four Corners region of southeastern Utah were carried on by local Mormon residents.

ELEVEN

THE MORMON SETTLEMENT OF SAN JUAN

1879–1887

By 1879, President John Taylor, new head of the Church of Jesus Christ of Latter-day Saints upon the death of Brigham Young in 1877, had directed a group of Mormons, mainly from the Iron County towns in southwestern Utah, to settle the San Juan region. The dual purpose was to promote friendly relations with the various Native American groups in the area, but also to establish a Mormon foothold in this southeastern part of Utah Territory, which was rapidly becoming populated with Gentile (non-Mormon) cattlemen. As with many of the larger-scale Mormon colonizing efforts, an exploring party was sent first to scout the way and to locate prime areas for settlement. The route taken was the already familiar road across Lee's Ferry and along the Echo Cliffs to Tuba City and then the trails followed by the San Juan gold-seekers northeast through the Navajo country to the Four Corners region.

This so-called San Juan Exploring Company left Paragonah, Utah, in mid-April, 1879. It was composed of thirty-six people, including the wives of two of the men and their eight children. At least two other men joined along the way through southwestern Utah. Not surprisingly, several members of the expedition took the time to carve their names at various camping places, adding their signatures to those of earlier passers-by. George B. Hobbs left his name, "G. B. Hobbs" and the year date of "1879" on the cliffside at the Granary Ranch in Johnson Canyon. According to the official "Camp Records," the company stayed here the night of April 23.[1] Just west of Willow Springs, in Arizona, there are three or four now illegible names, but a date of "Ma 7 1879" can still be made out. Again, the "Camp Records" indicate that parts of the expedition camped here from May 3 to May 7,[2] so the names are undoubtedly from the San Juan Exploring Company.

But as so often happened with the various colonizing groups to the Little Colorado region of northern Arizona earlier in the 1870s, most of the names left by the 1879 party were at House Rock Spring. Here, Robert Bullock, Edward F. Davis, John T. Gower, Thomas S. Bladen, George Urie, Kumen Jones, and James J. Adams all carved their names. Bullock and Jones also added the notation "Of Cedar City" to theirs, while Gower and Bladen were the only ones to include a date, "Apr. 25, 79." This agrees with the official "Camp Records."[3]

According to the "Camp Records" the exploring company arrived at the San Juan River on May 31, 1879. They remained on the San Juan for some two and a half

G. B. Hobbs, 1879.
Johnson Canyon, Utah.

R. Bullock of Cedar
(City). House Rock
Spring, Arizona.

J. T. Gower, T. S.
Bladen, Apr. 25th, 79.
House Rock Spring,
Arizona.

George Urie, E. P. Davis,
K. Jones of Cedar City.
House Rock Spring,
Arizona.

months, exploring up and down the river and some members even traveling as far as the Abajo Mountains and into southern Colorado. At Seventeen Room Ruin on the south bank of the river, two of the party left their names close by that of E. A. Barber's from 1875. Like him, John L. Butler and Hamilton M. Thornton carved only their names, no date, but both are listed on the

official roster of the 1879 exploring company.[4] They must have incised them at that time, as both of these men, upon returning to their homes near Panguitch, Utah, did not return to the San Juan with the colonizing mission the next year.

A site for the future colony was chosen on the north bank of the San Juan near the mouth of Montezuma Creek, cabins were built, and farming areas were cleared. The major part of the exploring company left on August 19, traveling north by way of Recapture Creek and intercepting the old Spanish Trail southwest of the La Sal Mountains. They then proceeded to follow that long-established route back to the southwestern Utah towns. The Davis and Harriman families, along with one other man, stayed at

Montezuma to prepare the way for the coming colonizing expedition.

Almost immediately upon the return of the exploring company, the so-called San Juan Mission was prepared to start out for the new settlement area at Montezuma. The southern route by way of Lee's Ferry and the Navajo country was deemed too dry and too dangerous, while the northern route via the old Spanish Trail was too long and too time-consuming. The first major contingents of the mission company were to leave the Utah towns by the latter part of October, and they wanted to be on the San Juan before winter fully set in. Therefore, a more direct "short-cut" was decided upon by way of the new community of Escalante, which would take them across the Colorado River midway through the length of Glen Canyon and then through the almost unknown landscape of the huge triangle of land lying between the Colorado and San Juan Rivers.

The trials and tribulations of what has become commonly referred to as the Hole-in-the-Rock expedition have been thoroughly documented in various sources. Suffice to say here that what was supposed to be a six-week trek turned into a nearly six-month ordeal, much of it during the dead of winter and through some of the most rugged canyon and plateau country of the region.

During this extended period of time, the almost 240 colonists might be expected to have left many inscriptions along their journey, but such is not the case. It probably comes down to the fact that simply existing and surviving took most of their time and energy. The inscribing of names and dates was definitely not a priority.

The first groups of the mission company arrived at the village of Escalante, Utah, in the early part of November. Working their way southeast along the base of the Kaiparowits Plateau, the now scattered wagons arrived at Forty-mile Spring by mid-month. This site was the major expedition headquarters for more than three weeks, until the first part of December. Many inscriptions can be found carved on the rocks around the spring and also at Dance Hall Rock a mile and a half to the northwest, but none are from the Hole-in-the-Rock expedition. If there ever were any, they have either weathered off or been obscured by more recent names.

Between Forty-mile camp and the brink of Glen Canyon, road-making had to be done almost the entire way, and progress was therefore much slower. Also, much blasting, rock excavation, and fill-work had to be done on the steep, narrow crevice leading down from the canyon rim to near the

J. L. Butler,
July 23, 1879.
Near Bluff, Utah.

H. M. Thornton,
July 23, 1879.
Near Bluff, Utah.

river bank. This is what came to be known as the famous Hole-in-the-Rock. For over a month, from mid-December until the latter part of January, this work went on. At the very top of the Hole, on the right-hand side, is a much weathered carving stating simply, "Decker, 1880." There were five separate families of Deckers on the trek, all from Parowan, Utah, and all related.[5] This is the only remaining inscription known from the San Juan Mission on the west side of the Colorado River.

While work on the Hole was taking place, four men were chosen to scout the way for the upcoming route east of the river clear to Montezuma on the San Juan. Many years later one of these four, George B. Hobbs, wrote an account of their journey. In it he says, "Night overtaking us, we camped in this small canyon [a short tributary of Butler Wash]. . . . I cut my name in the rock with the date I was there, not knowing that I would survive the journey."[6] This inscription was found in May 1960 by a group of local residents. It reads, "Geo. Hobbs, Jan. 1, 18[80]."[7]

The accompanying date is interesting historically, as Hobbs indicates that he scratched it on the wall of the gulch on December 27. Hobbs wrote his account in 1917, thirty-seven years after the fact, so he may have been off somewhat in his memory.

Or, he possibly was unsure as to the exact date at the time he incised it in 1879–80. It is known that he did, in fact, leave the inscription while on his way to Montezuma, as on the return trip the four scouts followed a trail along the bank of the San Juan River, crossing Butler Wash about two miles south of the inscription site.

By January 25 the road down through the Hole-in-the-Rock was pronounced complete, and a crude ferry boat, capable of transporting two wagons at a time, had been constructed. From January 26 until the first of February the mission company crossed the river.[8] Egress on the eastern side was by way of comparatively shallow Cottonwood Canyon. About a mile from the river the road passed a towering, almost vertical wall of sandstone. Here, with the perilous descent of the Hole and the dangerous crossing of the Colorado behind them, many members of the expedition did take the time and effort to leave a record of their passing. Before the rising waters of Lake Powell reservoir flooded the site, a historical survey crew from the University of Utah made a listing of these inscriptions about 1962.[9]

There were at least thirteen names, five of them with dates, carved into the base of what was named Register Rocks. They were "E. L. L. [Edward L. Lyman], Jan. 29, 1880,"

"C. E. Walton, Jan. 27, 1880," "E. Z. Taylor, Jan. 30, 1880," "J. Smith [there were three different Smiths in the company whose first name began with the letter 'J'], Jan. 30, 18—," "James W. Pace, 1880," "J. C. D. [James C. Dunton]," "J. F. B. [Joseph F. Barton]," "D. A. S. [David A. Stevens]," "J. E. S. [Joseph E. Smith]," "W. R. [William Robb]," "J. R. Robinson," "C. I. D. [Cornelius I. Decker]," and "S. C. G. [Sidney C. Goddard]."

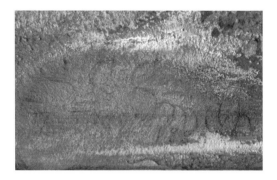

Some five weeks of arduous toil later, two members of the mission company scratched their names and the date next to a prehistoric petroglyph at an ancient Anasazi cliff dwelling on the north side of Castle Wash.[10] They were "E. L. Lyman" and the same "J. Smith" who had left his name back at Register Rocks. This is known because the "handwriting" is clearly the same. The date is "March 5, 1880."

Due to water and grazing limitations the company was strung out in separate groups, as is shown by an inscription that was left by "S. S. Smith" on "March 10 1880." It is inside of a small cave that is just three miles farther east from the cliff dwelling site.[11] This was more than likely left by Silas S. Smith, Jr., as his father, the president and leader of the San Juan Mission, had returned to Salt Lake City for additional supplies and materials on December 15, 1879. He did not rejoin the company until mid-May, 1880, after they were already settled on the San Juan River.

Much of the second week of March was spent in building a road down the treacherous east side of Clay Hills Pass, the only crossing for miles in either direction of the barrier of the Red House Cliffs.[12] Near the top of the old switchbacks, carved into a rounded rock boulder beside the roadway,

E. L. L., Jan. 29, 1880. Glen Canyon, Utah. Special Collections Dept., Marriott Library, University of Utah.

C. E. Walton, Jan. 27, 1880. Glen Canyon, Utah. Special Collections Dept., Marriott Library, University of Utah.

J. Smith Jan. 30, 18--. Glen Canyon, Utah. Special Collections Dept., Marriott Library, University of Utah.

S. S. Smith, March 10, 1880. Near Clay Hills Pass, Utah.

*Make Peace With God.
Clay Hills Pass, Utah.*

*J. Smith, W. Hutchings,
March 28, 1880. Near
Bluff, Utah.*

are printed the words "Make Peace With God." The carving is not dated, but it has a weathered appearance and is usually attributed by historians and writers to the Hole-in-the-Rock expedition.

By the end of March the company had finally worked its way to the north bank of the San Juan River at the mouth of Comb Wash. Along the low cliff bordering the river two more of the expedition members incised their names and the date into the rock. One was the ubiquitous "J. Smith" and the other was "Wm. H. Hutchings." The mission company camped nearby for several days while a road was cut up onto and over the barrier of Comb Ridge by way of what was called San Juan Hill.[13] The accompanying date with the Smith and Hutchings names is "March 28, 1880."

The ascent of Comb Ridge, aside from the Hole-in-the-Rock, was the steepest crossing of the trek and proved almost too much for the worn-out wagon teams. Most of the accounts left by members of the San Juan Mission describe in almost heartbreaking terms the toil of climbing San Juan Hill.[14] Thus, it is not surprising to find carved into a low rock wall at the top the large block letters stating, "We Thank Thee Oh God," words from a still popular Mormon hymn.

By the end of the first week in April,

most of the company had reached the flat river-bottom area just east of Cottonwood Wash. Although the intended settlement site at Montezuma was only some eighteen miles farther, the mission simply ground to a halt. Here most of them would settle. Not far to the east, near the mouth of Recapture Creek, the inscription "J. [John] H. Pace, Apr. 17, 1880" is still to be found. This was only eleven days after the San Juan Mission arrived at Cottonwood Wash.[15]

At the suggestion of William Hutchings (he of the inscription back at the foot of San Juan Hill), the new settlement was called Bluff City. Later this name was shortened to simply Bluff, supposedly by some of the more optimistic settlers to avoid confusion with Council Bluffs, Iowa, on the Missouri River, which was also referred to as "Bluff City." Bluff remains today a small town on the north bank of the San Juan River and even enjoyed a spurt of growth in the latter years of the 1990s. However, the originally chosen site upstream at Montezuma, though it did attract a few settlers, was mostly abandoned after disastrous floods in 1883 and 1884.

Overcrowding and the lack of arable farmland led to major changes within a few years. The basic economy of Bluff gradually changed more and more to livestock. In

1886 the so-called Bluff Pool was organized, and over a thousand head of cattle were trailed into the area from the Mormon towns west of the Colorado River. Representative of these new Mormon cattlemen was the Redd family, who remain important in the livestock industry of San Juan County even up until the present time. Lemuel H. Redd, Sr., one of the original Hole-in-the-Rock pioneers, did not settle in San Juan permanently, but his eight sons eventually did. One of them, Benjamin,[16] left his name and the date carved in the canyon wall just west of the mouth of Recapture Creek. It reads, "B. F. Redd, Apr. 17, 1891."

In the spring of 1887 a number of families from Bluff and the San Juan River were directed by Church authorities to settle at a site farther north at the foot of the Abajo Mountains, though the Mormon settlers, taking their cue from preceding prospectors, referred to them then, as now, as the Blue Mountains. This Blue Mountain Mission settled at two sites within six miles of each other on two branches of Montezuma Creek at the eastern side of the Abajos. The southern one became the settlement of Verdure, while the other was eventually named Monticello. Verdure is now only a small cluster of ranches, but today Monticello is a thriving town of about two thousand people.

J. H. Pace,
Apr. 17, 1880.
East of Bluff, Utah.

B. F. Redd,
Apr. 17, 1891.
East of Bluff, Utah.

TWELVE

MOAB AND GREEN RIVER

1874–1897

The founding of the towns of Moab and Green River, located in Grand and Emery Counties respectively, was not like that of most of the other southern Utah communities. Green River had its basis as a railroad town, though later in its history agriculture became an important part of the economy. Moab did have a more typical beginning, as a farming and cattle center. However, both had their roots as Gentile settlements, neither town being established as a result of "calls" by the Church of Jesus Christ of Latter-day Saints. While Mormon settlers did come to both Moab and Green River, they were not the first residents.

The location of the town of Moab is the direct result of the site being a crossing place of the Colorado River on the old Spanish Trail. Above and below this point the river flows through what were at the time nearly impassable canyons, but coming up from the southeast is the wide, open length of Spanish Valley, named, obviously, from its being traversed by the old Spanish Trail. To the northwest the somewhat rugged, but relatively short and passable, Moab Canyon provides an egress to the more open region lying near the Book Cliffs and Tavaputs Plateau.

Thus the locality had been visited by Native American, Spanish, Mexican, and early

American travelers for centuries. Spanish Valley, sometimes referred to as Grand Valley by early settlers because of the bordering river, and the locale for the modern town of Moab, was even settled, temporarily as it turned out, by the Mormon Elk Mountain Mission in 1855 (see chapter 5). However, it lasted less than a year. The so-called "modern" history of Moab, therefore, can be said to have begun in the mid-1870s.

In 1874, Crispen Taylor, from Juab County, Utah, came to Spanish Valley after talking with James and John Ivie, members of the short-lived Elk Mountain Mission. He evidently liked the prospects and returned with two nephews and a small herd of cattle the following year. But like the 1855 party, they were soon forced out by the local Utes. In the spring of 1876 brothers George and Silas Green, also from Juab County and friends of the Taylors, made a similar attempt. However, their luck was even worse. The next year a search party located the body of Silas, though no trace was ever found of George. It has always been supposed that they were killed by Indians.

Later, in the summer of 1877, the first residents actually settled in Spanish Valley. A mulatto, William Granstaff, and a French-Canadian trapper, Felippe Duran, took possession of the old 1855 Mormon "fort."

They raised a small garden and also ran a few cattle, supposedly remnants of the Green brothers' herd. That fall the Maxwell, McCarty, and Ray families all arrived in the valley, camping in the vicinity of the old fort until the following spring.[1] During their stay on the Colorado River that winter, some of the group may well have explored northward into the rugged area of sandstone fins and knobs making up today's Arches National Park. Two inscriptions are very lightly scratched on the inside of what is known as Indian Head Arch, both reading, "C. R., 1878." These possibly are a record of a member of the Ray family.

There is no doubt, however, that members of the Maxwell and McCarty families did leave their names and the year date carved at Kane Springs when they moved on with their livestock from Spanish Valley to the range on the southern slopes of the La Sal Mountains.[2] The site, which was originally spelled "Cane" because of the reed grasses growing around the moisture-saturated ground, had long been a watering and camping spot along the old Spanish Trail. Over the years scores of travelers have left their names and the date on the prominent nose of sandstone south of the spring area that now houses the tourist attraction of "Hole N' Rock." Behind some screening trees, the carvings of "P. Maxwell, 1878" and "McCarty Tom" can still be found.

The extended Maxwell, McCarty, and Ray families, all interrelated by marriage, had heard of the livestock possibilities of the Spanish Valley and La Sal Mountain region when Cornelius Maxwell passed through the area along the old Spanish Trail while on a trip to the mining areas of southwestern Colorado in 1873. They were Gentiles, and after some difficulties with their Mormon neighbors in the Grass Valley area of central Utah, had ultimately decided to move to the more remote southeastern part of the territory. Philander Maxwell, who left his first initial and name at Kane Springs, was a son of Cornelius. Tom McCarty, the other inscriber, was the brother-in-law of Lettie Maxwell, a sister of Philander.

More than a dozen individuals and

families came to Spanish Valley to settle in 1878 and 1879. In the latter year the growing community became a stopping point on the recently established mail route between Salina, Utah, and Ouray, Colorado, and when it was granted a post office in March 1880, the name Moab was adopted, from an ancient region in the Bible supposedly meaning the "far country."[3] That this was not a "new" name, however, is evident from an inscription left on Courthouse Rock, several miles north of the town. Lightly scratched on the west side of the huge sandstone monolith is the following: "B. B. Turner, Moab, Ut, July 1879." There were several Turner families that lived in the Moab area during the 1880s and 1890s.

In the winter of 1880–81, Crispen Taylor, this time with three of his nephews, brought some three thousand head of cattle to Spanish Valley. Each of the Taylors claimed homesteads in Moab, but, needing a summer range for their stock, also built some line cabins on the eastern side of the La Sal Mountains not far from the Maxwells, McCartys, and Rays. With this trio's some two thousand head of livestock, the Moab region was now definitely cattle country on a large scale. That fall Crispen's older brother Norman, recognized head of the Taylor clan, came to Moab to settle with

his two wives, three married sons and their families, and more than a dozen other younger sons and daughters.

The large Taylor family became influential and respected leaders in the region and remain so in Moab and Grand County today. Several miles north of town on Courthouse Rock is an inscription left by an "M. A. Taylor, Oct. 26, 1890." Not far past the west side of the Colorado River, two large rock slabs are leaning together in such a way as to form a crude shelter. On the inside, carved at the early date of "Apr 78," is the name "Ray Taylor." However, according to Samuel Taylor, long-time editor of the Moab newspaper, these are no known relatives of the Norman Taylor family.[4]

In 1885 the Pittsburgh Cattle Company, organized by a group of Pennsylvania financiers, bought the cattle and ranches of the Maxwell, McCarty, and Ray families, as well as a couple of other smaller outfits on the south side of the La Sal Mountains. There is evidence that the new company soon ran over ten thousand head of cattle in the region. Like their predecessors, the Pittsburgh Cattle Company ran their stock up on the south slopes of the mountains in the summer and down in the northern part of Dry Valley in the winter. But they must also have at least examined the Lockhart Basin

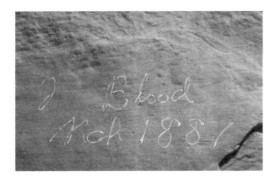

and Lockhart Canyon region draining west-ward to the Colorado River.

On the upstream side of the mouth of Lockhart Canyon is a panel of prehistoric Anasazi petroglyphs, accompanied by several historic inscriptions. One of these was very lightly scratched into the rock by "James C. Blood" in "Mch. 1887." Close by is an equally faint scratching that can, with careful scrutiny, be made out to read, "[illegible] Savage Mch. 1887." From 1885 through the mid-part of 1887, James Blood served as ranch foreman for the Pittsburgh Cattle Company,[5] while Jehiel V. Savage was cattle foreman.[6]

Like Moab, the town of Green River is situated near the crossing of that stream by the old Spanish Trail. It, also, has long been an important spot geographically and histor-ically speaking. The comparatively low and relatively flat area of several miles stretching between the Tavaputs Plateau and Gray Canyon to the north and the ever-deepening Labyrinth Canyon to the south was origi-nally known as Gunnison Valley. Along here is the only easily accessible crossing place of the Green River for many miles. This has been the case since Spanish times up even to the present day.

Thus the Salina-Ouray pack mail route, in operation from about 1878 to 1883 between

the southern Utah communities and the min-ing camps of southwestern Colorado, used the Green River crossing. A mail relay station was established on the west bank under the super-vision of a man by the name of Blake. The first permanent settlers arrived in the fall of 1879, and the railroad crossed here in 1883. For several years there was some confusion as to the actual name of the town. The postal designation was Blake, or Blake City, after the postmaster, but the railroad stop was named Green River, or Green River City. In 1895 the post office was changed to match the railway name, but was spelled Greenriver, one word, to distinguish it from the town of Green River, Wyoming. The return to the present-day name of Green River, two words, was made sometime in the 1930s.

The first settlers who came in October 1879 included the family of Thomas Farrer. Originally from the Sevier Valley, Utah, he and his sons had traveled that summer to western Colorado and southeastern Utah to look over the prospects for settlement. Com-ing back from Colorado into Utah between the Abajo and La Sal Mountains, they found themselves in Spanish Valley and what was soon to be the town of Moab. They stayed in the area for some time before heading out for Green River. This latter place, they ultimately decided, was where they would locate.

James C. Blood, Mch. 1887. Canyonlands National Park, Utah.

Peter Westenskow,
June Th.7, 1881.
San Rafael Swell, Utah.

Carl E. Jensen,
June Th.17, 1881.
San Rafael Swell, Utah.

The Farrers planned to run sheep, and believed that if they settled in the Spanish Valley–Moab area it would be too difficult to get the wool and mutton to market with two major rivers, the Grand (Colorado) and the Green, to cross. They also noted, as the eldest son, John T. Farrer, wrote in later years, that the valley ". . . [had a] perpendicular wall [of cliffs] around it and only one place to get in, that [only] the width of a wagon."[7] This is a good description of the so-called Jumping-Off Place, a ledge of rock all but blocking exit to the north on the west side of the river. The modern highway has been blasted through this barrier, located just to the north of the entrance to present-day Arches National Park. However, a sharp eye can even now pick out remnants and traces of the old route making its way up the steep, boulder-strewn slope to the right of the highway.

About halfway up the slope, one large boulder has a still plainly seen inscription carved into its uphill side. It reads, "J. T. Farrer, July 29/79." This carving was evidently put there by John T. Farrer, son of Thomas Farrer, while he, his father, and brothers were still in the area before they left for Green River. J. T., as he was always known, later owned and operated a general store and saloon that was Green River's

chief business establishment for some twenty-five years. He also ran the ferry across the river until a wagon bridge was finally constructed in 1910–11.

Farrer also wrote that even in 1879 they had heard there was the prospect of a railroad being built from Pueblo, Colorado, into Utah, and that after the family reached Green River and examined the location, they were convinced that if it was to be built it would come through there.[8] Their surmise proved to be correct. The original plans of the Denver & Rio Grande Railway called for the line to extend westward from Green River, following in general the route of the old Spanish pack trail. Upon reaching Salina, Utah, it would then turn north to the Great Salt Lake Valley. Accordingly, surveys were made of the proposed route across Castle Valley and through the San Rafael Swell, and by the early summer of 1881 grading for the railroad was being done along many stretches.

Through the heart of that portion of the San Rafael Swell lying to the north of the San Rafael River, the old Spanish Trail and the new railroad grade crossed Buckhorn Flat.[9] On the north side of the flat, near the base of Cedar Mountain, several large rock boulders are grouped together. Local residents in the nearby Castle Valley communi-

ties refer to them as Railroad Rocks, from the fact that most of the dozen or so inscriptions that have been carved into their sides come from the time of the railway grading. They are dated from June 6 until June 16, possibly representing a camp of some sort here at the time. Most of the names, Peter Westenskow, Carl E. Jensen, E. Miller, Adolph Axelsen, and Bert Fredericksen, can be traced to Castle Valley towns. Some of the local residents were evidently hiring out to the railroad to supplement their farming and ranching incomes.

As a final note, it must be stated here that the proposed line west from Green River, through the San Rafael Swell and Castle Valley, and over the Wasatch Plateau to Salina, did not come to pass. The newly reorganized Denver & Rio Grande Western Railroad did cross the Green River and passed through the town of Green River in the spring of 1883, but during the preceding year track had ultimately been laid from the Great Salt Lake Valley via a new route over Soldier Summit, down Price Canyon, and eventually southward toward Green River. The connection of the two railheads was made on March 30, with the first regular passenger runs beginning out of Denver on April 7 and out of Salt Lake City on April 8.

E. Miller, J. T. Daly,
June 7th, 1881.
San Rafael Swell, Utah.

Adolph Axelsen,
June th.6, 1881.
San Rafael Swell, Utah.

THIRTEEN

SILVER AND GOLD

1879–1899

In the Navajo country of northern Arizona, tales of a hidden silver mine spurred exploration of the wild tangle of canyons and plateaus lying between Monument Valley on the east and the solitary dome of Navajo Mountain to the west. It began with stories and accounts that have now become so entwined that it is difficult, if not impossible, to separate fact and truth from myth and legend. The ultimate explorations were searches for what became known variously as the Lost Merrick-Mitchell Mine, after its supposed finders, or the Lost Pesh-la-ki Mine, from the Navajo word for "silver."

Basically, the beginnings of the account go something like this. In late 1878 or early 1879 a man by the name of Merrick (though it is also given as Merritt or Myrick), in passing through the Navajo nation from Fort Wingate, New Mexico, to Lee's Ferry, Arizona, had discovered three crude smelters where the natives had been melting silver from silver ore. Collecting some samples, he subsequently had them assayed with a result of 90 percent silver. By the beginning of 1880, Merrick had gained a partner named Mitchell (first name either Ernest or Herndon, depending on the version of the story), and during the first week in January they were on their way from Mitchell's father's trading post on the San Juan River, near the

mouth of McElmo Creek, to try to find the source mine of the silver ore. In late January or early February, when nothing had been heard from the two prospectors, a search party from the Mancos Valley area of southwestern Colorado traveled to Monument Valley. At the bases of the two square-shaped buttes that now bear their names, the bodies of the unfortunate men were found. Local Navajos and Paiutes blamed one another. Later, toward the beginning of March, another party, which included young Mitchell's father, returned to the valley to recover his body for burial.[1]

Supposedly, one or both of these groups made a hurried search for the mine itself, but without success. However, according to Gladwell Richardson, son of the owner of Inscription House Trading Post, in the late 1920s he saw an old set of initials and date at nearby Inscription House ruin. It read, "J. E. H. March 1880."[2] Perhaps this person was a member of the second party. Unfortunately, this inscription is no longer to be found at the site. In the latter half of the 1920s the National Park Service ordered all "graffiti" removed from the ruin, and evidently the 1880 inscription was one of those that was taken off.

Other prospecting parties now entered the region, searching for the reported "lost"

mine. In the winter of 1880 a large group of twenty-two men from the Mancos Valley area set forth to hunt for it. One member, according to the writings of Louisa Wade Wetherill, was her father, Jack Wade.[3] He and his companions prospected the country around Monument Valley, but after several weeks no clue to the location of the mine was found. They finally returned to Mancos in February 1881.

On the wall of the shallow alcove sheltering Tse Ya Toe Spring, a dozen miles south of Navajo Mountain, there are many names and dates carved and drawn. One of these is that of "B. I. Bill." Immediately below is the year date, "1880," pecked into the rock with some sort of metal tool. Since this large prospecting party was in the region for several weeks, they could easily have gotten to Tse Ya Toe, some thirty to forty miles west of Monument Valley. By 1882 a Benjamin Bill was a freighter in northern Arizona,[4] and he possibly was a member of the 1880–81 prospecting party.

According to a short autobiography written by prospector and miner Cass Hite later in his life, in the autumn of 1881 he and four companions left the mining camps of southwestern Colorado and "went down to the Rio San Juan and into the Navajo country to hunt for a silver mine."[5] Though his

companions are not named, one of them was probably an M. S. Foote. That name and a date are found carefully incised at two different locations in the Navajo region. The first, dated "Dec. 16," is close to Peach Spring in Tsegi Canyon, along one of the two major Native American routes between Monument Valley and Navajo Mountain. The other, carved twelve days later, is some twenty to twenty-five miles to the northwest in Forbidding Canyon, almost in the shadow of Navajo Mountain.

The small party must have headed back to Colorado soon after this last December 28 inscription was made, as both Hite and Foote are listed in a Durango newspaper article as being members of a much larger prospecting group that left that town on January 17, 1882, "bound for Navajo mountain in search of treasures of gold and silver."[6] In fact, Foote is titled as "Captain" of the expedition. Thus, it was probably on this trip that today's Nokai Canyon, a southern tributary of the San Juan River and crossed by the other of the two routes between Monument Valley and Navajo Mountain, was at that time named Foote Canyon. This was very likely the largest and best equipped prospecting party to enter the Navajo country. The nearly one dozen inscriptions that were left by at least six of its

B. I. Bill, 1880. South of Navajo Mountain, Utah.

M. S. Foote, Dec. 16, 1881. Tsegi Canyon, Arizona.

G. E., Tsegi Canyon, Arizona.

Geo. E(mmerson), AP 1, 1882. Near Navajo Mountain, Arizona.

Geo. Emmerson, Ap. 1, 1882. Navajo Mountain, Arizona.

members are a good indication of the extent of area covered in the time they were out, from the middle of January until the first part of April.[7]

On the way either to or from Navajo Mountain, "J. A. Duckett" and "G. E." left their names and initials on the same cliffside near Peach Spring in Tsegi Canyon that M. S. Foote had the previous December. In the Durango newspaper article these two inscribers were named as Joe Duckett and George Emerson (*sic*).[8] Joseph A. Duckett was later a prospector and miner in the Abajo Mountain–White Canyon area of San Juan County, Utah. The latter years of his life were spent living a hermit's existence in Montezuma Canyon, east of the town of Monticello, where he died in 1933.

That the "G. E." is, in fact, the initials of this George Emerson (*sic*) is borne out by two other inscriptions he left carved farther north. Along Cottonwood Wash, just a short distance southeast of Navajo Mountain, is found "Geo. E," the "G" and the "E" done in exactly the same style as the initials in the Tsegi. About four miles to the west, carved into a line of rocky cliffs ringing the foot of Navajo Mountain itself, he left a more complete signature plus the date. It reads, "Geo. Emmerson, Ap. 1, 1882." Once again, the "G" and "E" of the first and last names are

done in the identical manner as the corresponding letters of the other two inscriptions. There is no doubt that George Emmerson (note two "m's" in the name) left all three carvings.

The southernmost of the two cross-country routes led southwest from the Monument Valley area to Marsh Pass and the mouth of Tsegi Canyon. Turning north up the Tsegi to Peach Spring, it then followed the branch of Bubbling Spring Canyon for a distance before climbing steeply out over the plateau northwest toward Navajo Mountain, crossing Piute Canyon on the way by what is still known as the Upper Crossing. Just before reaching the mountain Cottonwood Wash would be encountered, and there, on the opposite side of the rock projection from the "Geo. E" inscription is another, reading, "G. Miller, 1882." A George

Miller was also listed as a member of the prospecting expedition.[9]

According to an April issue of the Denver newspaper, about half of the large party back-trailed homeward over their original route, while the others stayed behind to continue the search for the silver mine. This latter group then traveled south before heading back to Durango,[10] thus passing by the eastern rim of the Navajo Canyon drainage. Evidently at least a few of the prospectors descended into the Neetsin area of the gorge and over into the next tributary canyon to the north, as indicated by inscriptions that they left behind.

Just as the 1861 group of Mormons before them had been, these later prospectors must have been attracted by the prehistoric cliff dwelling of Inscription House, as at least two of them left their names and the year date in the small but comparatively deep cave on the left side of the ruin. On one wall, carved low down toward the floor, is "C. M. Cade, A.D. 1882." Near the back, and evidently printed with wet charcoal, is "N. C. Young, 1882." Both a Cash Cade and a Notley Young are listed in another April Denver newspaper article as being among those ". . . explorers who remained behind to look further for the hidden treasures of the Navajo mountains. . . ."[11] Less

than a mile to the north, over a low saddle into Toenleshushe Canyon, is the remnant of a small Anasazi ruin at the base of the flanking sandstone wall. Next to it, on the cliffside, the same two men again printed their names with charcoal, along with a third, "L. Reed." This was Lorenzo Reed, also listed as one of the party who remained behind.

By the middle of April all of the various groups of the divided expedition had

G. Miller, 1882.
Near Navajo Mountain, Arizona.

C. M. Cade, A.D. 1882.
Inscription House ruin, Arizona.

N. C. Young, 1882.
Inscription House ruin, Arizona.

L. Reed.
Near Inscription House ruin, Arizona.

G. M. Miller. South of Navajo Mountain, Utah.

Hite, Sept. 19th, A.D. 1883. Glen Canyon, Utah. Special Collections Dept., Marriott Library, University of Utah.

returned to Durango. Just as Merrick had done back in 1879, they reported finding "old Indian smelters,"[12] but saw nothing of the fabled mine itself. However, a month later, on May 17, seven of the prospectors left yet again for the "Navajo mountains and Monumental Valley country . . ."[13] to work a promising copper deposit in the upper reaches of what is still today called Copper Canyon. It had reportedly been discovered by Cass Hite in March during the extensive late winter–early spring expedition. The newspaper account of this latest search gave the names of four of the seven prospectors, but not the other three. Perhaps one of the latter was "H. L. W.," as no one listed for the 1881 and earlier 1882 prospecting parties had those initials. The initials, plus a year date of "1882," were formerly seen in the late 1920s at Inscription House ruin in Navajo Canyon,[14] though this inscription is no longer to be found today.

One of the members of the prospecting group who was listed was George M. Miller, who had left an inscription along Cottonwood Wash just southeast of Navajo Mountain earlier in the year. At Tse Ya Toe Spring his name, "G. M. Miller," can be found carved into the soft sandstone twice and then written with charcoal. Very likely these could represent three separate visits by

Miller, as the May newspaper article stated that the members of this latest exploring party had all been through the Navajo Mountain and Monumental Valley country once before and "some twice."[15] Cass Hite would have been one of these and possibly George Miller was another.

That this third tour was also unsuccessful is indicated by the fact that that fall Hite was again back in the region, this time actually living with the local Navajo band of Hashke'neini (more commonly spelled Hoskininni) for nearly a year in an effort to learn the whereabouts of the supposed mine. According to Hite, the chief refused to show him the location of the silver because of fear for his safety from other members of the band. However, Hashke'neini would, in a magnanimous gesture, guide Hite to the Glen Canyon area of the Colorado River, where gold could be found in abundance in the sands and gravels.[16] Much more likely is that the Navajo simply wanted to rid himself of a no-longer-welcome visitor.

Arriving in the early fall of 1883, Hite settled on the west bank of the Colorado near the mouth of Trachyte Creek. On some shallow overhanging ledges between North Wash and Trachyte were several inscriptions, a couple of which dated back to the 1800s. One of these read, "Hite, Sept. 19th, A.D.

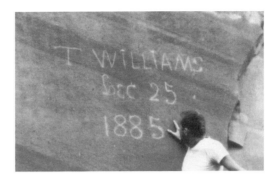

1883." According to a biography of Glen Canyon prospector and river-runner Bert Loper, by Pearl Baker, Hite told Loper that he had carved his name on the rock "the next day after I got there. . . ."[17]

Hite did, in fact, find placer gold in Glen Canyon, and his discoveries resulted in a mild rush of prospectors and miners into the region. The quest had now shifted from silver to gold, and until the end of the 1880s probably several hundred men searched the canyon and its tributary streams. They left close to one hundred historic inscriptions carved and written on the rocks and walls, the vast majority of which, unfortunately, are now deep beneath the water of Lake Powell reservoir. Two of the earlier inscriptions were left around Christmas of their respective years, that being a time, of course, when lonely prospectors often thought of home. "C. R." carved his initials into the rock on the east side of the Colorado across from the mining camp of Hite on "26 Dec. 1884," while "T. Williams" inscribed his name in large letters near the mouth of the Escalante River on "Dec. 25, 1885."

Cass Hite became a fixture in Glen Canyon gold prospecting for the next thirty years, until his death at his cabin on Ticaboo Creek in 1914. One interesting inscription, still to be seen along Capitol Gorge in Capitol Reef National Park, seemingly offers an intriguing commentary about him. In large, deeply cut block letters are the words "Cass Hite Is A . . ." followed by the pecked outline of a horse and a man face to rear. It does not take much of an imagination to decipher the probable meaning of the concluding drawing: "Cass Hite Is A horse's ass!"

This inscription-drawing is signed "T. C., March 7, 1885." Farther along the wall of the narrow canyon, high up among the many other names and dates that give this portion of Capitol Gorge its title of the Pioneer Register, is a difficult-to-see message left by "Theodore Christensen," and dated "febuare [sic] 18, 1885." According to the biography written by his daughter, "T. C." and "Theodore Christensen" were the same person.[18] The second inscription is unusual both in the fact that it is inscribed in long-

Theodore Christensen ... febuare 18, 1885. Capitol Reef National Park, Utah.

Wm. Bright. J. M. Butler. Came to river, 1889. Left Apr' 5th, 1901. Glen Canyon, Utah. Special Collections Dept., Marriott Library, University of Utah.

hand, not printed, and gives not only a name and date, but what the inscriber was doing, where he was from, where he was going, and what was the result. This remainder of the message reads, "Prospector, Gunnison Ut, henre mounte [*sic*] or bust." A short, later addition, evidently on the return, states, "busted by god."

Theodore E. Christensen and his family had come to the Sevier River valley of Sanpete County in the fall of 1854 and had settled near where the town of Gunnison would be founded a few years later. All of his adult life he was an entrepreneur, dabbling in many different interests and fields, including mining speculation. Thus, he was not a true "prospector" in the usual sense, but rather was scouting out already established prospects for investment purposes. According to his daughter, on this same trip her father also went from the Henry Mountains on down to Glen Canyon and the Colorado River.[19] There, Christensen must have encountered Cass Hite, and any possible mining deals evidently did not work out, to say the least.

During the 1880s, and to a smaller extent in the 1890s, gold was found in Glen

Canyon all along the Colorado from the mouth of the Dirty Devil River to Lee's Ferry. But it was extremely fine, literally gold "dust," and it was very difficult to recover by the ordinary placer methods of panning and sluicing. However, enough was taken out to encourage a small, but steady, flow of hopeful prospectors into the region. Typical, then, would have been the inscription carved with many others into the long canyon wall on the western side of Hall's Crossing. It read, "Wm. Bright. J. M. Butler. Came to river, 1889. Left Apr' 5th, 1901."

William Bright also left his name carved at least twice on the so-called Fort Moqui prehistoric ruin just below the mouth of White Canyon, one carving dated 1889, the other 1890. John M. Butler, or Jack as he was known during his years in Glen Canyon, was described as being an old Cincinnati Southern Railway "tunnel man." In other words, he was proficient in the use of dynamite for blasting purposes, of little use in placer mining, but a definite asset for a hard-rock miner. This, then, undoubtedly came in handy in the working of his lode-vein claim on the eastern side of Mount Ellen in the Henry Mountains. Like several other Glen Canyon miners, Jack Butler spent the cooler winter months down along the Colorado River and the warmer summer

season up in the mountains. He eventually became enough of a fixture in the region that two streams were named for him and remain so on modern maps: Butler Creek, an eastern tributary of the Colorado between Hall's Crossing and the Escalante River, and Butler Wash, on the southeastern flank of Mount Ellen.

Toward the end of the year 1892, stories began to trickle out that rich gold placers had been found on the San Juan River deep in the canyons below the town of Bluff.[20] By January 1893, the subsequent rush was at its height. Representative of the many prospectors who poured into the region were "D. Fairbanks" and "T. T. Howe." Their names are painted onto a canyon wall of a northern tributary of Sulphur Creek, west of Capitol Reef. Though undated, directly beneath the pair of names is also painted, significantly enough, the words, "San Juan Gold." Nothing else of these two men has been learned.

Within a few weeks, however, the San Juan "excitement" had already begun to die down. Most prospectors found that the stories had been exaggerated and that the few good claims had already been taken up. It was reported that one disgruntled individual described his feelings on a sandstone boulder at Navajo Spring along Comb Wash. "One

Hundred Dollars Reward For the Damned Fool Who Started the Gold Rush."[21] Unfortunately, this caustic epithet was destroyed when the nearby modern road was blasted through the top of Comb Ridge to facilitate automobile travel between the towns of Bluff and Mexican Hat, Utah.

But, as in Glen Canyon, a few die-hard prospectors and miners stayed on along the San Juan canyons up until the end of the century. One such example was the extended Honaker family. Augustus C. Honaker, the family head, had come to Mancos, Colorado, from Missouri in 1881, and within the next two years was joined by the families of several brothers and sisters. He was a freighter, operating between Cortez, Colorado, and Bluff, when the San Juan gold rush began. Almost immediately he and his relatives joined in, staking claims in December 1892 and January 1893. They again filed on claims some eight miles west of Mexican Hat in 1894,[22] and in the spring of that year began construction of the Honaker Trail. This is a precipitous, 1,200-foot set of switchbacks, still in evidence today, that descends the canyon wall to Honaker Bar, a large gravel deposit along the San Juan River where the family ultimately mined some gold.

Various Honakers also left several inscriptions behind at different places along

the San Juan. A mile or two downstream from the mouth of Montezuma Creek can be found "S. W. Honaker, Jan. 18, 94," and in the canyon of Lime Creek, north of Mexican Hat where it cuts back into the heights of Cedar Mesa, can be seen "Henry Honaker, May 12, 1894." Silas W. Honaker was a brother of Augustus, while Henry A. Honaker was a nephew. At Seventeen Room Ruin, east of Bluff, are the faint scrawls of three Honakers, including "A. Honaker," probably Augustus himself.

The prospectors, then, and the miners were the first to make a thorough search of the main canyons of the Colorado and San Juan Rivers and the area around Navajo Mountain. Very likely they also examined every tributary gorge from its mouth up to at least the point where prospecting seemed probable of success. If these seekers after silver and gold found few good diggings, they did, literally, discover the canyons, exploring at close range the jumbled and intricate landscape of the heart of the Colorado Plateau region.

FOURTEEN

ARTIFACTS AND RELICS

1888–1897

Ever since the first Spanish conquistadors began making their entradas into what is now the American Southwest, they encountered the ruined dwellings of a prehistoric civilization that predated any of the indigenous native peoples then inhabiting the area. Some of these ruins still contained items of the now-departed people who, in the Colorado Plateau region in particular, are commonly known today as the Anasazi, a Navajo word meaning "ancient enemies." For over three hundred years such items as implements and tools of wood and stone, clay-fired pottery, reed baskets and sandals, and occasionally woven textiles, were found and appropriated as "souvenirs." It was not until the latter part of the 1800s that a few enterprising individuals began to collect these prehistoric artifacts and relics to sell for a profit.

In the Colorado Plateau region this practice began in the Mesa Verde area of the state of Colorado. To the Mancos Valley, lying at the northeastern base of the green, tree-covered mesa, came the family of Benjamin K. Wetherill in 1880. A few miles south of what would the next year become the town of Mancos, they established the Alamo Ranch and, like some of their fellow ranchers, encountered the prehistoric Anasazi ruins scattered along the canyon of the Mancos

River as it cut its way diagonally across the southern reaches of Mesa Verde. But it was not until the winter of 1888 that the discovery was made that would cause a significant change in their lives.

On a late December day the eldest Wetherill son, Richard, and his brother-in-law, Charles C. Mason, while searching for stray cattle on the southern-extending finger of Mesa Verde that would later be named Chapin Mesa, espied what they soon called Cliff Palace, the largest Anasazi cliff dwelling in the Southwest. After a cursory examination of the ruin, they split up to search for more sites.[1] The initials "R. W.," carved above a doorway in nearby Spruce Tree House, and the name "Mason," incised inside of an axe-groove at Bone Awl House across Soda Canyon east of Chapin Mesa, were undoubtedly left by Richard Wetherill and Charles Mason, but more than likely at a date sometime after that fateful December 18th and 19th.

Returning to their camp in Mancos Canyon, Wetherill and Mason ran across three friends: Charles McLoyd, John H. Graham (who went by his middle name Howard), and Levi C. Patrick, who were in the canyon trapping. They told them of their discoveries, and, upon being joined by one of Richard's brothers, John, the group returned to the ruins to try to make a collection of relics.[2]

R. W. Mesa Verde National Park, Colorado.

Mason. Ute Mountain Tribal Park, Colorado.

C. McLoyd. Ute Mountain Tribal Park, Colorado.

J. H. Graham, L. C. Patrick /3/89. Ute Mountain Tribal Park, Colorado.

They spent the winter of 1888–89 doing just that and also leaving behind inscriptions at the various sites they worked. On the cliffside to the left of what is sometimes called Nordenskiold House, on the eastern side of Chapin Mesa, is the carved name "C. McLoyd." Also on this side of the mesa, overlooking Soda Canyon, can be found "J. H. Graham" and "L. C. Patrick," this time with a date of "[Feb.]/3/1889."

In the spring the Wetherill brothers continued collecting on Chapin Mesa.[3] On the east side, again at Nordenskiold House, Clayton left the following inscription: "C. Wetherill, Mch. 21–1889." In May the amassed collection of cliff-dweller artifacts and relics was taken to Denver, where it was purchased by the Historical Society of Colorado.

It was now understood that such Anasazi paraphernalia could be very valuable. When

the Wetherills set out to make another collection in December of 1889, they decided to go at it as a business proposition. John Wetherill left his initials at a site on the western side of Chapin Mesa dated "1-26-90," but most of that winter was spent on farther to the west at what was later to be named Wetherill Mesa.[4] Several of the cliff dwellings there contain the simple inscription "Wetherill, 1890." This second collection was later sold to H. Jay Smith, art director of the Minneapolis Industrial Exposition.

By the spring of 1890, the Wetherills had examined over 180 houses. Many of these ruins, no matter how small or difficult of access, contain inscriptions. Typical is the following. Sometime in the early 1900s, according to a story later related by archeologist Alfred V. Kidder, he and Jesse Nusbaum, then superintendent of Mesa Verde National Park,

Butch Cassidy Was Here

were exploring cliff dwellings on the west side of the mesa. Seeing one high up on a canyon wall and making their way by a perilous route to it, they were sure that they were the first humans since the original Anasazi inhabitants to visit the precariously perched ruin. They were, therefore, dumbfounded when they looked inside and saw written on an upended slab of rock, "What fools these mortals be! R. Wetherill."[5]

In the winter of 1890–91, Charles McLoyd and the older of the Graham brothers, also named Charles, both of whom had been working for the Wetherills on Mesa Verde, decided to strike out on their own. They headed west in late December toward the tributary canyons of the San Juan River in southeastern Utah. In particular, they had heard stories that untouched prehistoric cliff ruins were to be found in Grand Gulch. From the first week in January until the end of March, the two men methodically searched the length of the canyon.

At many of the sites that McLoyd and Graham dug, one or both of them would leave their names and, occasionally, the date. Researchers in the 1980s discovered at least a score of inscriptions left by Charles Graham at different sites in Grand Gulch, while his partner, Charles McLoyd, left even more.[6] Most of the time they signed together, but a few times individually, and the majority of occasions the duo wrote with bullet lead or charcoal, rarely incising their names. Each of the times that they included a date with their names it was the year "1891."

Only twice did McLoyd and Graham include a month with their year date, and each time it was January. One is on the south side of Grand Gulch, between the tributaries of Step and Dripping canyons, and is "C. C. Graham, Chas. McLoyd, Jan. 1891." The other, written in charcoal only by "C. C. Graham" on the inside wall of the underground chamber at Perfect Kiva ruin, is dated "Jan. 11–91," the only one with a day date given. In his diary of the trip, Charles Graham briefly stated in his entry for that date, "11. Sunday. We worked in Cliff house No. 1. Graham Canon."[7] The name Perfect Kiva was not bestowed until much later in

the twentieth century, while "Graham Canon" is today the major eastern tributary of Grand Gulch known as Bullet Canyon.

McLoyd and Graham dug up enough artifacts, including mummified skeletons, to fill a wagon. From Bluff they were freighted to Durango, Colorado, where McLoyd then lived. There they were sold to Charles H. Green. The collection was later purchased by the Field Columbian Museum, now the Field Museum of Natural History in Chicago.

No doubt encouraged by their success, McLoyd returned again to Grand Gulch the following winter, 1891–92, but this time with Howard Graham. From dated inscriptions that they left behind, they evidently dug for the most part in the upper half of the canyon. Graham included both the month and day dates with the year date of "1892" on three of his four "J. H. Graham" signatures. At the site now called Kokopelli and the Dancers (after some nearby prehistoric petroglyphs) the date is "Jan. 7," at what was later called Cave 10, "Jan 31st," and at Turkey Pen ruin, "Feb. 18." McLoyd also left his name and the year date written in charcoal at Turkey Pen ruin, "Chas. McLoyd, 1892."

Two of the J. H. Graham inscriptions and one of McLoyd's also have "Durango, Colo." appended to them. The Graham family had come to Colorado from Indiana in

1879. In 1883 they homesteaded on the Los Pinos River, several miles east of Durango. Charles McLoyd, meanwhile, was a miner, rancher, and sometime fur trapper, who lived in the Los Pinos River valley near the small community of Bayfield and later in Durango. McLoyd and Graham sold their collection to C. D. Hazzard, a wealthy collector in Milwaukee, Wisconsin. Later it was split between the University of Pennsylvania Museum and what is now the Hearst Museum at the University of California–Berkeley.

McLoyd, with Charles Graham, returned yet a third time to southeastern Utah, during the winter of 1892–93. In an account written several years later, Graham said that on this occasion they went around the head of Grand Gulch and down Lake Canyon to the Colorado River. They then ". . . came back and went down White Canyon a little ways. . . ."[8] On the cliffside to the right of the upper level of Lightning House ruin in upper White Canyon is a faint charcoal inscription from this trip. It reads, "Graham & McLoyd, W.C., Nov 17/92." In this upper portion of White Canyon, in the northeastern section of today's Natural Bridges National Monument, are at least four other inscriptions left by McLoyd and Graham. The two left by McLoyd are undated, but the two of Graham's both have the year date "1892."

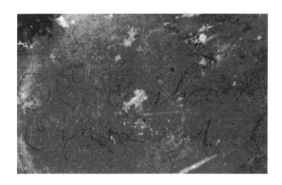

According to Henry L. A. Culmer of Salt Lake City, who visited the White Canyon natural bridges in the spring of 1905, there was also another pair of McLoyd/Graham inscriptions. In his diary entry for April 15, Culmer wrote, ". . . I spent some hours in the difficult task of making a sketch of the Caroline [now Kachina] Bridge; but was somewhat distracted by the cries of the rest of the party in their discoveries of the . . . hieroglyphics [prehistoric pictographs and petroglyphs] in the surrounding caves. . . . At the hieroglyphics or picture scratching or peckings was written the names of W. C. McLoyd and C. C. Graham 1892–3."[9] There is, in fact, an incised name and date pecked into the rock on the south side of the eastern abutment of Kachina Natural Bridge, but it reads only, "C. C. Graham, 1892."

Finding little success in the way of recoverable artifacts and relics in these other southeast Utah canyons, McLoyd and Graham returned once more to the already proven environs of Grand Gulch. There, sometime around the first of the year, they were joined by John Wetherill, who left his last name, "Wetherill," and the date, "Jan. 10, 1893," at what is now known as the Red Elk site. The resulting third McLoyd collection was sold to John B. Koontz of Aztec, New Mexico. Later it was purchased

by another collector and donated to the American Museum of Natural History in New York City.

Earlier, in the spring of 1892, a completely different sort of group entered the San Juan canyons of southeastern Utah searching for ruins and relics. This was a scientific expedition headed by archeologist Warren K. Moorehead, whose purpose was to obtain a collection of artifacts for the Peabody Museum of Harvard University. It was funded principally, however, by the *Illustrated American,* a weekly magazine.

From Durango, Colorado, the Illustrated American Exploring Expedition, as it was called, journeyed to the San Juan River and then westward to Bluff, Utah. Like many travelers before them, the exploring expedition stopped at Seventeen Room Ruin not far east of Bluff.[10] Scratched into the alcove

C. C. Graham, C. McLoyd. Grand Gulch area, Utah. Courtesy of Fred M. Blackburn.

C. C. Graham, 1892. Natural Bridges National Monument, Utah.

L. W. Gunckel, May 5/92, I.A. Survey. Near Bluff, Utah.

1892, Cold Spring Cave, I.A.E.E. Butler Wash, Utah.

M. C. L., 5/11/92. Butler Wash, Utah.

I. A. E. Exped. Butler Wash, Utah.

wall back of the line of rooms is found "L. W. Gunckel, May 5/92, I. A. Survey." Lewis W. Gunckel, from Dayton, Ohio, was the geologist for the group, which, as the inscription indicates, was also known as the *Illustrated American Survey.*

Just as the Wetherills, Patricks, McLoyd, and Grahams before them had done, the Illustrated American Exploring Expedition left carved inscriptions at many of the cliff-dweller sites that they visited. After establishing a base camp near Bluff, the majority of the men headed out on May 10 to Butler Wash and its cave ruins. The next day, some seven miles from the San Juan River, they climbed up to their first site in the steeply sloping eastern side of Comb Ridge. There, on a boulder near a pool of water, is carved "Cold Spring Cave," and underneath, "I. A. E. E," both still plainly visible today. In one of his articles for the *Illustrated American,* Moorehead wrote, "We named the place Cold Spring Cave, on account of the fine spring of cold, clear water. . . . It flows out . . . into a round clear pool."[11]

About five hundred feet to the right of the main part of the cave-alcove, near some ruin remains and a kiva, is another carving. It reads, "M. C. L., 5/11/92, Cinti, Ohio." Expedition leader Moorehead later wrote, "Mr. Maurice C. Longnecker from Cincin-

nati came on with the boys . . . and became one of our most valuable men."[12] Longnecker was not an original member of the expedition, but was a friend of Clinton Cowens, also of Cincinnati and the party's surveyor and topographical artist. Longnecker was extremely anxious to see the Southwest country, so Cowens brought him along.

Probably two days later, on the 13th, another cave-alcove was discovered less than a mile to the south. Carved into the sandstone wall near the cliff dwelling are two inscriptions. One reads, "I. A. E. Expedition," while the other proclaims, "Monarch's Cave." In one of the *Illustrated American* articles, Lewis Gunckel states, "We named it Monarch's Cave, for it must have been monarch of all it surveyed."[13] On the morning of May 14, according to Gunckel, they

discovered another cave site a few miles farther north as they worked their way up Butler Wash. Today can still be seen on the back wall the boldly incised name "Giants Cave." This, once again, is from the I. A. E. expedition of 1892, as Gunckel, in his article, goes on to say, "From its enormous dimensions we called it Giant's Cave. . . ."[14] Today, however, it is known locally by the equally descriptive title of Fishmouth Cave.

From the upper part of Butler Wash the party made its way eastward in to the head of Cottonwood Wash, and after searching the surrounding region for the next day or so, Gunckel led his small party back to Bluff. The modest collection of artifacts was sent to Professor Frederick W. Putnam at Harvard University, who, in turn, exhibited it the next year at the World's Columbian Exposition in Chicago.

Benjamin T. and Frederick Hyde, brothers and wealthy heirs to a considerable business fortune, had visited the Mesa Verde ruins the previous year and had arranged with Richard to lead an expedition to the Grand Gulch region in the winter of 1893–94. At the end of November 1893, Richard and a small group left Mancos, Colorado. At least four members of the party left inscriptions during the subsequent expedition, several of which include both the day and month dates. This has al-

lowed modern researchers to reconstruct with some accuracy the itinerary and movements of the expedition during its nearly four months in the field.[15]

Thus we know that by the following day the party had traveled some twenty to twenty-five miles to a western tributary then known as First Valley and today called Whiskers Draw. There, on the back wall of a small cave-alcove, one of the men, Harry French, wrote in charcoal, "H. French, Dec. 12–1893." W. H. French, though he was always known by his middle name of Harry, was a fellow rancher of the Wetherills in Mancos, having arrived at that town from Chicago, Illinois, in 1888.

The expedition examined five other alcoves in the vicinity before reaching what they called Cave 7, a couple of miles to the north in a fork of Whiskers Draw, sometime before December 20. James L. Ethridge, a cowhand on the Wetherills' Alamo Ranch near Mancos, carved his name and the date at Cave 7, where they dug for several days. Though partially obscured by more recent writings, "J. L. Ethridge, Dec 20, 1893," can still be made out.

Shortly after spending Christmas back in Bluff, the group headed out once more. This time they evidently went west a few miles before turning north up Butler Wash, as the

Giant's Cave. Butler Wash, Utah.

H. French, Dec. 12–1893. Cottonwood Wash area, Utah. Courtesy of Bruce Hucko.

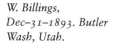

W. Billings,
Dec–31–1893. Butler
Wash, Utah.

Hyde Exploring
Expedition, 1/1/1894.
Butler Wash, Utah.

Wetherill, 1894. Grand
Gulch, Utah.

J. L. Ethridge,
Jan–23–94. Grand Gulch
area, Utah.

next inscription is found at what the expedition called Cave 10, today's Fishmouth Cave and Giant's Cave of the Illustrated American Exploring Expedition. On the back wall of the huge alcove is printed in charcoal, "W. Billings, Dec–31–1893." Wirt Jenks Billings, of Denver, Colorado, had been a visitor at the Wetherills' Alamo Ranch and was guided by them to the Mesa Verde ruins prior to 1891. The next day, of course, was New Year's, and printed in large charcoal letters on the side of a rock boulder spalled off of the alcove ceiling is the official name of the group as well as the date, "Hyde Exploring Expedition, 1/1/1894."

At least a couple of days were spent at Cave 10, Billings having the time to write in charcoal the following elegy to its former prehistoric residents at the rear of the alcove. "To inhabitants of this deserted place! Your bodies long ago returned unto the dust. Alas! You all are gone to come again no more!" Soon after, the expedition turned westward, and by the first part of January they had reached their goal, Grand Gulch.

Descending into the largest eastern tributary, Graham Canyon (today's Bullet Canyon), the party was at what they called Cave 14 by January 8. In his usual charcoal medium, Harry French again left his signature on the wall of the alcove back of the ruin now called

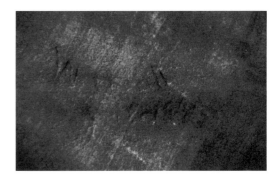

Perfect Kiva. Above a pair of prehistoric handprint pictographs, it is "H. French, 1/8/94." Also, scratched into an axe-groove on top of a fallen boulder was "Wetherill, 1894." Unfortunately, this latter inscription has been nearly obliterated by modern visitors.

The expedition apparently spent the better part of two weeks examining and digging in the several alcoves of Bullet Canyon, as James Ethridge left his name in what is now

called Burial Cave No. 3 reading, "J. L. Ethridge, Jan-23-94." It is clear, but rather faint, appearing to have been done with the lead bullet of a gun shell cartridge.

Within a day or two after the 23rd, the expedition reached the mouth of Bullet Canyon and entered Grand Gulch itself. At this point they split, Richard sending brothers Al and John down the canyon to explore for promising sites to dig, while the main portion of the party turned up the gorge. Al and John traveled fast, making only cursory examinations of the most likely alcoves, and so covered over thirty miles of lower Grand Gulch in the next few days. Inscriptions with the generic name "Wetherill" and the dates of January 25, 26, and 27 have been found at four different locations along this portion of the canyon. All are done in the same style and were obviously left by the two brothers.

While Al and John were scouting lower Grand Gulch, the rest of the expedition continued to travel slowly upstream, excavating alcove sites wherever encountered. At Green Mask alcove, just a short distance up a small eastern tributary now known as Sheiks Canyon, James Ethridge left his characteristic first and middle initials and last name with the date "Jan. 26, 1894," in the upper level of the ruin located there. Not more than a mile distant, in the main part of

Grand Gulch at what is today known as Cut-in-Two Cave from the mummified remains of a prehistoric human body dug up there, is a signature left by the group's other regular inscriber, Harry French. It is dated "1-29-94."

After Al and John Wetherill rejoined the main group, the party headed back down the canyon to explore and excavate in the undisturbed sites they had found. Two inscriptions carved at Wetherill Cave in lower Grand Gulch probably date from February. Here can still be clearly seen "1894, Wetherill" and "W. Billings, 1894." Just above the mouth of Rope Canyon, Ethridge left a bullet-lead inscription dated "Feb. 22, 1894." This is the last signature from the 1893–94 Hyde Exploring Expedition found in Grand Gulch, and though this does not necessarily mark the end of their explorations it must

have been close, as they were back in Bluff by the first part of March.

By April the over 1,200 items, both artifacts and human remains, were freighted back to the Alamo Ranch near Mancos, and after being sorted and catalogued they were crated and shipped to the Hyde brothers. The following year the collection was presented by the Hydes to the American Museum of Natural History in New York.

In the winter of 1894–95, two former members of the Hyde Exploring Expedition returned to the Allen Canyon area of upper Cottonwood Wash north of Bluff. Charles B. Lang and Robert Allan, both of whom lived in that community, joined with at least one other townsman, Franklin J. Adams, to make a collection of artifacts and relics for their own profit.[16] At Twin Caves, on the eastern side of Allen Canyon, is the charcoal-inscribed "Nov. 1894, C. B. Lang." At two other alcoves in the canyon, Lang again left his name, one with the added name of "R. Allan" and the other with "F. J. Adams." This small band of Bluff citizens evidently referred to themselves as the San Juan Exploring Expedition, as there is yet another inscription with the name "F. J. Adams," underneath which are the initials "SJEE."

One of the objectives of the 1893–94

Hyde Exploring Expedition had been the Navajo country of northern Arizona, but with the spectacular success that they had had north of the San Juan River, time did not permit their going there. Evidently, however, Richard Wetherill did lead a small group to this region the first part of 1895. According to an account written some years later by his brother John, Richard, brother Al, brother-in-law Charles Mason, and two other men left Mancos late in December and spent the next three months working their way south up Chinle Creek and then west along Kayenta Wash (today's Laguna Creek).[17] Evidently one of the two unnamed men was Richard's old friend from Denver, Wirt Billings, as a charcoal inscription reading, "W. Billings, Apr. 1895" is still to be found written on the wall of a small cave in a short, northern tributary of Laguna Creek

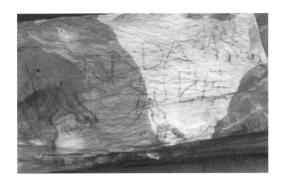

in Marsh Pass just east of the mouth of Tsegi Canyon. According to the official report of an archeological expedition sent to the region by the Peabody Museum of Harvard University in 1915, the charcoal name of Richard Wetherill was also noted along with that of Billings at that time.[18] Today, unfortunately, it has evidently weathered away, though the Billings name and the date are still quite plain.

The artifacts found during this trip to northern Arizona are the one major Wetherill collection of which nothing is known. To whom or where the relics went is a mystery. But the artifact and relic collecting continued. In the fall of 1896 a wealthy Harvard student, George Bowles, and his tutor, C. Edward Whitmore, arrived in Mancos wanting to see the surrounding archeological sites. Richard proceeded to convince them to fund and accompany another expedition to Grand Gulch.[19]

On this second expedition it was not as if they were exploring unfamiliar territory, but even so, Richard did send James Ethridge, the lone holdover from the first expedition other than Richard himself, on ahead early to scout the way. This was probably because the expedition was planning on entering the gulch by a different route from that used in 1894. The 1897 group would

come in by way of the eastern tributary they would call Wetherill Canyon, today's Kane Gulch. Just as he had done in 1893–94, Ethridge again this time left his name and a complete date in at least ten sites along Grand Gulch.

On this early reconnaissance, Ethridge inscribed his name and "December, 1896" at today's Split Level Ruin and at two other locations down the canyon. His last signature from this scout is dated "Jan. 16, 1897," at Turkey Pen Ruin. This is back upcanyon once again and was made on his way out of the gulch to join the main body of the expedition, which had left Mancos about January 13 and Bluff on the 18th.

One of the group's main camps was at what they called Cave 6, today's Split Level Ruin alcove. Charles Mason left his only inscription in Grand Gulch here, "C. C. Mason." Found here, also, are the initials "W. E. E., 1897." No one in the party had these initials, and they undoubtedly stand for "Whitmore Exploring Expedition," after Teddy Whitmore, financier for the expedition.

Much time was spent excavating in the surrounding area, as evidenced by inscriptions left at nearby sites. Ethridge gave a date of "Feb. 15, 1897" at their Cave 10 (today's Red Man Cave). Another member

F. J. Adams, SJEE. Cottonwood Wash, Utah. Courtesy of Winston Hurst.

W. Billings, Apr. 1895. Marsh Pass, Arizona.

of the expedition, Orian H. Buck, left "O. Buk [sic]." Buck was a farmer and rancher from McElmo Canyon, west of Mancos, and had been a freighter for the Hyde brothers between Mancos and Pueblo Bonito in northwestern New Mexico. Carved into the hardened mud at Cave 9 (Kokopelli and the Dancers alcove) are two sets of initials, "R. W." and "M. W." These were very likely incised by Richard Wetherill and his newlywed wife, Marietta, who had come along to keep the records of the expedition.

February found the group up Graham (Bullet) Canyon, where the ubiquitous James Ethridge signed in on "Feb. 23, 1897" at what is today known as Burial Cave No. 2. Perhaps it was at this same time that the name "Wetherill" was printed, also with bullet lead, at nearby Jail House Ruin. Some ten miles farther down Grand Gulch, at the site known today as Kokopelli and the Mountain Sheep after some nearby Anasazi petroglyphs, is "J. L. Ethridge, Feb. 25, 1897." While this is the last dated inscription from the expedition with the specific day and month given, there are a few more found nearby at the Pollys Island rincon and several others still to be seen farther down the canyon in the vicinity of what is now known as Bannister Spring.

In an alcove in the northern part of the

Pollys Island rincon, close to the expedition's Camp 5 and written in charcoal, is "L. Carson, 1897." This latter was left by Levi Carson, originally from the Animas River valley north of Durango, Colorado. He was one of the packers and horse wranglers for the expedition.

Near Collins Canyon the expedition halted and Richard made the decision to leave the gulch, return to Bluff, and then head south across the San Juan River to continue explorations in the Navajo country. Sometime in March the party split up into three groups. James Ethridge, William Henderson, and Clayton Wetherill were sent to examine the alcoves of Moqui Canyon, which flowed into the Colorado River west of Grand Gulch, while George Bowles was dispatched with Charles Mason and Orian Buck to explore the ruins of Mysterious Canyon, which drained the area south and west of Navajo Mountain. Meanwhile Richard and the remaining men (Marietta stayed in Bluff) would work their way south along Chinle Wash and then west up Laguna Creek to Marsh Pass. There, the three groups would meet, sometime in April.[20]

An inscription reading, "C. Wetherill, 4–4–97," formerly located in an alcove-cave in the lower part of Moqui Canyon, was undoubtedly left by the first group, while a

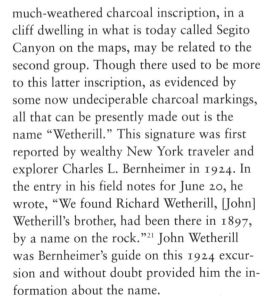

Wetherill. Grand Gulch area, Utah. Courtesy of Bruce Hucko.

L. Carson, 1897. Grand Gulch, Utah. Courtesy of Winston Hurst.

C. C. Mason, Mancos. Keet Seel ruin, Arizona.

G. W. Hairgrove, 1897. Tsegi Canyon area, Utah.

much-weathered charcoal inscription, in a cliff dwelling in what is today called Segito Canyon on the maps, may be related to the second group. Though there used to be more to this latter inscription, as evidenced by some now undeciperable charcoal markings, all that can be presently made out is the name "Wetherill." This signature was first reported by wealthy New York traveler and explorer Charles L. Bernheimer in 1924. In the entry in his field notes for June 20, he wrote, "We found Richard Wetherill, [John] Wetherill's brother, had been there in 1897, by a name on the rock."[21] John Wetherill was Bernheimer's guide on this 1924 excursion and without doubt provided him the information about the name.

In April the three groups reunited as planned at Marsh Pass, and the entire party then proceeded northward up Tsegi Canyon (not to be confused with Segito Canyon some twenty-five to thirty miles to the northwest). The party reached the large ruin of what was later named Keet Seel, as indicated by an inscription left on the sloping roof of the huge alcove above one of the room blocks. Written in charcoal, it says, "C. C. Mason, Mancos." Just around the corner of the canyon to the north is another large alcove, known as Turkey Cave. Here, also written in charcoal, is "R. Wetherill," with some additional faint markings below. According to a 1969 National Park Service archeological report, this lower portion at that time read, "Mancos, Colo., 1897."[22] A mile or so beyond, high on the west wall of the canyon, is perched a small cliff dwelling. On the sandstone to the left of the ruin, printed with charcoal in large block letters is "G. W. Hairgrove, 1897." George Hairgrove

R. Wetherill,
April 1897. Tsegi
Canyon, Arizona.

C. C. Mason, 1897.
Tsegi Canyon, Arizona.

R. Wetherill, 1897.
Tsegi Canyon area,
Arizona. Courtesy of
Andrew L. Christenson.

was one of the cooks in charge of the "kitchen" for the expedition.

Back in the main part of the Tsegi, where Bubbling Spring Canyon enters from the west, Richard Wetherill and Charles Mason left their names in charcoal in a cave-alcove much as they had done back at Keet Seel. About six miles farther on, up the extension of the Tsegi named Long Canyon at the cliff ruin known as Ladder House, is the last Whitmore Exploring Expedition inscription, Richard's now familiar charcoal signature, "R. Wetherill, 1897."

By early May the Wetherills were back in Mancos. The resulting collection of artifacts and relics was finally purchased by the Hyde brothers and, like their 1893–94 collection, was eventually donated to the American Museum of Natural History. This was the last major archeological expedition in the Colorado Plateau region whose principal intent was the sale of the prehistoric items found for a monetary profit.

FIFTEEN

THE RIVERS

1879–1897

From the time of the second Powell expedition in 1871–72, it was some seventeen years before the next voyage by boat down the canyons of the Green and Colorado rivers took place, and seven years before the canyons of the San Juan River were navigated. During the 1880s short stretches of the rivers and canyons of the Colorado Plateau region were traveled by watercraft of various kinds, but only for relatively short distances. Primarily these trips were to get to or from placer claims and mining camps. While the larger streams would seemingly provide watery roads to traverse the rough and broken canyon and plateau county, the presence of whitewater rapids, especially in Cataract, Marble, and Grand Canyons, prohibited such endeavors.

With the tapering off of the silver and gold excitement of the 1870s in the San Juan Mountains of southwestern Colorado, at least one enterprising prospector thought to test the possibilities of placer deposits that had been washed down the river from the mountains. Reportedly in 1879, Emery L. Goodridge, originally from Akron, Ohio, left Animas City and descended that river to the San Juan near Farmington, New Mexico. From that point he made his way down the length of the San Juan River to where it flowed into the Colorado and then down that stream to Lee's Ferry.

By 1882, Goodridge was back once more repeating his boat voyage of 1879. This time, however, he departed from the town of Bluff and, instead of making any gold claims, filed on a claim for *oil* near the present-day town of Mexican Hat, Utah.[1] Less than a mile up the river from the modern highway bridge, opposite the mouth of Gypsum Wash on the south side, is a plainly carved inscription reading, "E. L. Goodridge, Nov. 2, 1882." This is very close to where he filed his petroleum claim, and the date very likely represents the claim date. However, Goodridge did not bring in his first successful oil well until 1908.

The first river voyage down the canyons of Grand River (now the Colorado) from the Grand River Valley of western Colorado to The Confluence in today's Canyonlands National Park was not made until 1889. At that time Denver mining engineer Frank C. Kendrick was hired to conduct a survey for a water-level railroad along the Grand River to its junction with the Green. Later, another party would continue the survey down the Colorado. Kendrick and four other men in one boat left the town of Grand Junction, Colorado, on April 1, floating the some 160 miles of the Grand River except for a twelve-mile portage around the rapids of Westwater Canyon.

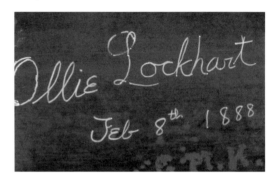

E. L. Goodridge,
Nov. 2, 1882.
Mexican Hat, Utah.

John E. Brown,
Jan. 9, 1887.
Canyonlands National
Park, Utah.

Ollie Lockhart,
Feb. 8th, 1888.
Canyonlands National
Park, Utah.

One month later, the surveying party was some 130 miles downstream. At that point, in his notebook entry for May 2, Kendrick says, "... we found a little valley coming in from the south [sic] where it appears some few cattle come to water, the first below Moab. On a large rock on the east [sic] side of the canon there are many Indian inscriptions. . . . Also the names of many cowboys written in 87 & 88."[2] Kendrick's "little valley" is now known as Lockhart Canyon and actually comes in to the Colorado River from the east. On the north side of the canyon's mouth can still be seen the many prehistoric petroglyphs carved there as well as the cowboy names.

Two of the 1887 names are those of James C. Blood and Jehiel V. Savage (see chapter 12). Another, that of "John E. Brown," is dated "Jan. 9, 1887." He, too, was a cattleman and had come to the Blue (Abajo) Mountain region of southeastern Utah in 1879. He worked as a cowhand for Joshua "Spud" Hudson and then, after 1883, for Green Robinson on the southern slope of the La Sal Mountains. In January of 1887, Brown was working for the Pittsburgh Cattle Company, which had bought out Green Robinson and the other La Sal ranchers.

The 1888 inscription mentioned by Kendrick is an intriguing one. It reads,

"Ollie Lockhart, Feb 8th, 1888, Silverton, Colo." Incised into the sandstone cliffside near the others, it is scratched so lightly that it is now nearly invisible except when the sun is at the proper angle. Oliver Lockhart was not a cattleman, he was not a miner, and, as the inscription indicates, he was not even a local resident. Historical records existent today indicate that he did, in fact, live in Silverton, Colorado, in 1888 and was the county clerk. It is believed by researchers that he was simply on a "one-time vacation-adventure,"[3] though his brief presence did result in the naming of the canyon after him.

The only other inscription associated with the 1889 Kendrick voyage is important, historically speaking, as it is the only one known left by the survey party itself. On the western side of the "Y" formed by the junction of the Grand and Green rivers with the

Colorado, the following inscription is carved into a large boulder: "Sta. 8489+50, D.C.C. & P.R.R., May 4th, 1889." This marks the last survey station of the Kendrick trip. From this point they laboriously rowed their boat some 117 miles up the Green River to Blake (now the town of Green River), Utah. In his notebook entry for that date, Kendrick states, "At mouth of Green we mark a large red sand stone lying in the forks of the Green & Colorado. . . ."[4] The initials in the inscription stand for the name of the proposed rail line, the Denver, Colorado Canon & Pacific Railroad.

Soon after the Kendrick portion of the railroad survey, the main party arrived at Green River from Denver. This group was led by chief engineer Robert B. Stanton, though also accompanying the expedition was the president of the D.C.C. & P.R.R. company, Frank M. Brown. Sixteen men in six boats pushed off on May 25, 1889, to float down the calm waters of the Green River. They would pick up the survey where Kendrick had left off at The Confluence, which was reached four days later.

Of the several inscriptions left along the Green and Colorado rivers by trapper and trader Denis Julien in the mid-1830s (see chapter 3), the first discovered was by the Brown-Stanton party in the lower part of Cataract Canyon. It was cut into the rock face of the cliff on the east side of the river, and in Stanton's notebook entry for June 20, he says, "About a quarter of a mile above our camp . . . I discovered . . . the following, '1836, D. Julien.'"[5] Modern historians and researchers have determined that Julien was originally a fur trader from the St. Louis area of the Mississippi and Missouri rivers and had come west to New Mexico by 1827.[6] In 1836 he was associated with the Fort Uintah trading post of Antoine Robidoux in the Uinta Basin area of northeastern Utah.

Upon reaching the mining camp of Hite on June 24, the railroad party was split into two groups. Brown, Stanton, and five of the men would push on as rapidly as possible to the town of Needles, California, on the lower Colorado river, making an "eye survey" as they went. William H. Bush, the assistant engineer, and four others would remain and carry the much slower instrumental survey through Glen Canyon to Lee's Ferry and from there return to Denver.[7] By July 14 this latter group reached what later river runners named Mystery Canyon and what has since then been renamed on modern maps Anasazi Canyon, some five miles below the junction of the San Juan and Colorado.

Sta. 8489+50 D.C.C. & P.R.R., May 4th, 1889. Special Collections Dept., Marriott Library, University of Utah.

1836, D. Julien. Cataract Canyon, Utah. Gift of P. T. Reilly.

On the upstream side of this tributary canyon, Bush's group left the only record of their trip. Each of the men carved their names, "W. H. Bush," "E. [Edward] Coe," "E. [Edward] Howard," "C. [Charles] W. Potter," and "G. [George] A. Sutherland." Three of the five also left the date, "7/14/1889." There is also incised "D.C.C. & P.R.R. Survey," and "No. 2." This last refers to their boat, the number two boat of the original six.

Meanwhile, the other eight members of the survey (three men were left at Hite) continued on down the Colorado through Glen Canyon, leaving Hite on June 26 in three boats. They arrived at Lee's Ferry on July 2, and after a week of rest and reprovisioning their supplies, embarked on down Marble Gorge toward the Grand Canyon. On the morning of the 10th, shortly after breakfast, the boat carrying President Brown was upset by a wave, and Brown was drowned. The men stayed at the eddy near the mouth of Salt Water Wash all that morning, hoping to recover the body, but without any success.

In the afternoon, while the others went on downstream a short distance to make camp, Peter Hansbrough remained at the accident site on the left bank. It was at this time that he chiseled the inscription still to be seen today on a low rock ledge not far above river level. In his diary entry for July 10, Franklin A. Nims, the photographer for the expedition, stated, "Mr. Hansbrough stayed and cut in the face of the cliff, 'F. M. Brown, Pres. D.C.C. & P.R.R. was drowned July 10, 1889, opposite this point.'"[8]

That night the decision was made to continue the survey on down the river. In Stanton's notebook entry for July 13, he says, "We call this Lone Cedar Rapid from a large cedar tree under which we eat lunch."[9] The location was some twenty-three or twenty-four miles below Lee's Ferry, and on the left bank today is still to be seen Stanton's "cedar tree," in actuality a juniper. Carved with neat letters into the trunk is "H. McD." This was clearly left during the lunch-break by Harry McDonald, a Glen Canyon prospector and miner who had been hired at Hite when three of the expedition's

members had left the survey. He had come west in the years following the Civil War, ranging from Montana to Arizona, and had engaged for the most part in herding cattle, prospecting, and mining. When hired by Brown in 1889, he had been in Glen Canyon for over two years.

Two days later, on July 15, tragedy struck the survey expedition once again. In the fast water just below what today is known as 26-Mile Rapid, one of the boats was upset and the two occupants, Henry Richards and, ironically enough, Peter Hansbrough, were both drowned. This time there was no question of going on. The survey was discontinued, and the party exited Marble Gorge by way of a tributary, South Canyon. Back in Denver, Stanton convinced the railroad company to complete the survey. He was retained as chief engineer and became a member of the board of directors. By December 6 he was back at Hite with, including himself, four veterans of the first voyage, eight new men, and three new boats.

The reorganized survey left the mouth of Crescent Creek (today's North Wash) on December 10, 1889, and quickly dropped some five miles down to the mining settlement of Hite. In his diary entry for that date, expedition member William H. Edwards wrote, "Crossed the river after lunch and explored

some Aztec [*sic*] ruins."[10] This was the prehistoric Anasazi pueblo that was known to the Glen Canyon prospectors as Fort Moqui, and that had been visited by the Powell expedition nearly twenty years earlier. Scratched into one of the sandstone building blocks of the structure was, before the rise of the Lake Powell reservoir, "W. H. Edwards, [Dec.] 10, 89." Edwards was from Watertown, New York, and had come to Denver, Colorado, in 1887. He was hired as a boatman for the railroad survey by Robert Stanton in 1889 after responding to an ad for the position that had been placed in a local newspaper due to a last-moment vacancy.

On December 23, some seven and a half miles above the Paria River, the expedition halted their survey and pulled on down to Lee's Ferry, where they camped for the next five days over Christmas. A little over two miles upriver from the ferry crossing, sitting back away from the river at the base of the eastern cliffs, is a large, deep alcove known today as Hislop's Cave. Deeply carved into a huge, fallen mass of rock is "1889 Hislop." Jonathan Hislop was the assistant engineer on this second expedition. He more than likely left this inscription on December 27, as William Edwards's diary entry then states, "We cross the river [to the eastern side] and finish the survey down to this point [Lee's Ferry]."[11]

1889 Hislop. Above Lee's Ferry, Arizona.

P. M. H., 1889. Grand Canyon National Park, Arizona. Courtesy of Grand Canyon National Park.

On December 28 the survey expedition departed on the Colorado River and into Marble Gorge. By January 16, 1890, they had carried the survey down to what would later be called President Harding Rapid. Late in the afternoon the remains of Peter Hansbrough were discovered, some eighteen miles downstream from where he had drowned the previous July. The next day the body was buried at the base of the towering canyon wall on the left bank. In his notebook entry for the 17th, Stanton says, "We covered his grave with marble [*sic*] slabs, and [Langdon] Gibson cut on the cliff beside it 'P. M. H., 1889.' "[12] Meaningfully, Edwards in his diary states, "Most of the men felt reluctant to cut the name as he [Hansbrough] was the one to cut Brown's name in the rock [on the first trip], and he was the next one to lose his life."[13]

The expedition reached the mouth of Diamond Creek, in the lower part of the Grand Canyon, on March 1, and spent a week and a half at this spot. A wagon road followed the creek some twenty-five miles south to the town of Peach Springs, Arizona, on the Atlantic and Pacific Railroad (now the Burlington Northern Santa Fe), and there was even a rough, clapboard "hotel" a short distance up the creek to serve tourists who made their way here to the "bottom"

of the Grand Canyon. By the 5th the survey was completed down to this point, and the next day three of the men were sent out from the expedition, as their boat had been wrecked farther up in Grand Canyon. One of these was Leo G. Brown, a boatman on the survey from Denver.[14] Sometime before he left, possibly on March 5, he cut his name and the year date on the canyon wall of Diamond Creek about a hundred and fifty yards back from the river. Still quite plain today, it simply says, "Leo G. Brown, 1890."

Stanton finally disbanded the survey at Yuma, Arizona, on the 30th. In brief, the water-level railroad down the Colorado River was never built. Stanton himself, however, intrigued by the placer gold deposits the expedition saw throughout Glen Canyon, did return there in 1897 to head an ultimately unsuccessful gold-dredging operation. Tales of valuable mineral deposits were also brought back to Denver by other members of the expedition.

In 1891, James S. Best, a Denver financier and capitalist, headed an expedition down the Colorado River to locate a reported silver lode seen near the mouth of Bright Angel Creek in the depths of the Grand Canyon. Incredibly, the boat venture to this spot commenced at Green River, Utah, presumably to

prospect for any other likely mineral deposits along the way. Tellingly, when the eight-man expedition shoved off on July 15, four of the members were veterans of Stanton's survey party of the previous year. The boats descended the smooth waters of the Green River, reached The Confluence on the 20th, and entered the rapid-strewn stretch of Cataract Canyon the next day. On the 22nd their number-one boat was capsized and pinned against a rock partway through what is now called Mile-long Rapid.

The expedition spent over a week at this spot in a futile attempt to salvage the boat.[15] During this time several of the men left various inscriptions carved into the rock boulders on the western bank of the river. One reads, "Col. Grand. Canyon. Mg. & Impt. Co. July 22, 1891, No. 1 Wrecked." Close by on another boulder is the terse statement, "Camp No. 7, Hell To Pay, No. 1 Sunk & Down." The Colorado, Grand Canyon Mining and Improvement Company was the official name of Best's endeavor, while this was the expedition's seventh campsite since leaving Green River. And there was certainly "Hell to pay," as the eight-man expedition was now reduced to only one boat and the loss of more than half of its supplies.

Individual names left on the rocks included "Js. Best," "H. McD.," "W. H. E.,"

Leo G. Brown, 1890. Diamond Creek, Arizona. Gift of P. T. Reilly.

Camp No. 7, Hell To Pay, No. 1 Sunk & Down. Canyonlands National Park, Utah.

Js. Best. Canyonlands National Park, Utah. Courtesy of Canyonlands National Park.

W. H. E. Canyonlands National Park, Utah.

and "Jacobs." Harry McDonald and William Hiram Edwards had both been members of the Stanton survey, while John H. Jacobs, an "oarsman" for the Best Expedition, was on the river for the first time. Though the latter two names are still quite clear today, the first two were largely destroyed during a rock slide about 1983. The "H. Mc." of McDonald's name remains, however.

Jacobs. Canyonlands National Park, Utah.

D, GC, M, I, Co., 1891. Cataract Canyon, Utah. Gift of P. T. Reilly.

Jno. Hislop, 1889, '90, 1891. Glen Canyon, Utah. Special Collections Dept., Marriott Library, University of Utah.

Through the remainder of Cataract Canyon and on to Hite, five of the men walked along the shore, while the other three in the boat would ferry them from one side of the river to the other whenever the canyon walls would close in next to the water. In the lower part of the canyon those in the boat saw the inscription that had been discovered by Robert Stanton back in 1889. In a narrative account William Edwards says, ". . . as we rowed slowly down the river along the left [east] wall we saw what appeared to be a name cut or picked in the rock. On rowing closer we find '1836, D. Julien.'"[16] Just to the right of the Julien signature, before inundation by Lake Powell reservoir, could be seen the initials "D, GC, M, I, Co., 1891," evidently standing for Denver *(sic)*, Grand Canyon, Mining & Improvement Company."

On August 4 the Best expedition finally reached Hite, where they rested and obtained additional supplies during the next two days.[17] Like many prospectors, miners, and river travelers before them, some of the men crossed the Colorado to visit the pueblo ruin of Fort Moqui. Jonathan Hislop left his third and final entry scratched in small letters on the south wall of the building, reading, "Jno. Hislop, 1889, '90, 1891." A professional civil engineer by training and living

in Denver, he had been a transitman on the Brown survey, assistant engineer and right-hand man for Stanton, and was now chief engineer with Best. In later years he helped in the building of the Yukon-Alaska railroad following the Klondike gold rush.

After prospecting at several riverine gravel bars through Glen Canyon, the water voyage ended at Lee's Ferry when it was realized that only one suitable boat was not sufficient to transport the men of the expedition down the large rapids of Marble Gorge and the upper Grand Canyon to Bright Angel Creek. It was deemed more practical to reach the creek overland, so Best left for Kanab to secure the necessary pack and riding horses. He was then called to Denver for a conference with the other stockholders in the company, leaving the men of the expedition at Lee's Ferry for a full two months, from their arrival on

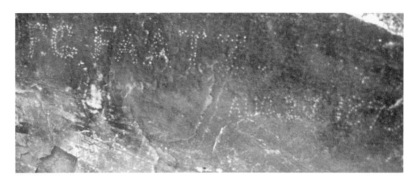

E. Kane, Aug. 20, 91.
Lee's Ferry, Arizona.

McC. Photo. Near Lee's
Ferry, Arizona.

F. G. Faatz,
Aug. 27, 1892.
Canyonlands National
Park, Utah. Special
Collections Dept.,
Marriott Library,
University of Utah.

August 14 until October 15. They camped at the old stone trading post and fort, built by the Mormons in 1874.[18]

On the left side of the front doorway, one of the expedition members, Elmer Kane, pecked "E. Kane" and the date, "Aug. 20, '91," on the face of one of the building stones of the structure. He was from central Pennsylvania and had come west in 1882 to Colorado, where he prospected and mined. Hearing about the Brown survey expedition, he traveled to Denver but arrived too late to catch on. However, he remained in that city, and when Stanton returned after the drownings in Marble Gorge, they met. Kane was hired as a boatman for the second trip and served in the same capacity as an "oarsman" on the Best expedition.

To pass the time some of the men explored the canyons, cliffs, and plateaus surrounding Lee's Ferry. In a lengthy narrative account he wrote many years later, the photographer for the expedition, James A. McCormick, tells of a trip he made up the Pairea (Paria) creek to where a well-used trail led to the top of the enclosing cliffs. He goes on to describe the "hieroglyphics" found on some of the broken rocks at the foot of this trail.[19] These prehistoric petroglyphs can still be seen today, as well as a carved inscription reading, "McC. Photo."

Ultimately, five members of the expedition, via horseback, traveled up onto Buckskin Mountain (the Kaibab Plateau) to Bright Angel Creek. Upon examination, the reputed silver vein turned out to be worthless, and the party was broken up.

In the following year, 1892, two individual prospectors, perhaps inspired by the Best expedition, descended the canyons of the Green and Colorado Rivers from Green River, Utah, to Lee's Ferry, Arizona, in the expectation of finding gold. Both had been hired, or "grubstaked," by mining companies in Salt Lake City. Neither kept a diary or journal account of his trip, but based on dated inscriptions each left carved along the Colorado River in Cataract Canyon, Friend G. Faatz probably departed Green River in early August,[20] while George M. Wright left that same town late in August or early

G. M. Wright,
Sep. 16, 1892.
Canyonlands National
Park.

F. G. Faatz,
Nov. 16, 1892. Above
Lee's Ferry, Arizona. Spe-
cial Collections Dept.,
Marriott Library, Univer-
sity of Utah.

G. M. Wright,
Nov. 16, 1892. Above
Lee's Ferry, Arizona.
Courtesy of Stan Jones.

September.[21] Like many river runners before
and since, each stopped to look over the
rock-strewn stretch of Mile-long Rapid.
There, Faatz left "F. G. Faatz, Aug. 27,
1892," while Wright later recorded "G. M.
Wright, Sep. 16, 1892."

Wright left at least three other signatures
in lower Cataract and Glen Canyons, all
dated and indicative of his slow progress
downstream as he prospected. He must have
traveled faster than Faatz, however, as a little
over ten miles above Lee's Ferry both of them
carved their names together and with the
same date, "Nov. 16, 1892." Oral accounts
told by Faatz to his family in later years indicated that he had been overtaken by Wright
just a few days earlier, and that they had then
traveled on together down to Lee's Ferry. A
Wright inscription there is dated "Nov. 17."
Faatz remained around Lee's Ferry for over a
year, before he married a Mormon girl and
settled down in Sanpete County, Utah.
Wright, too, stayed in the area for a couple of
years, then drifted farther south in Arizona to
new mining prospects.[22]

In 1893, William H. Edwards, of both
the Stanton and Best expeditions, was back
on the river. That spring he persuaded
friends in Denver to lease a thirty-five-foot,
open-decked steamboat near Green River for
the purpose of transporting tourists down to

The Confluence and on to the head of the
rapids in Cataract Canyon on the Colorado.
In April, Edwards and two others made a
trial run,[23] and an extremely faint paint-scar
inscription today marks their farthest point
down the canyons. On a large talus boulder
at the extreme southern end of what is now
known as Spanish Bottom can be barely
made out the words "1st Steamer Major
Powell, Mar. 24–'93."

Major Powell was the name given to the
steamboat, after, of course, the intrepid river
explorer of 1869 and 1871–72. No longer to
be seen at all now, but barely visible to a
historical survey team from the University of
Utah in the early 1960s, were the names
"W. H. Edwards," "H. F. Howard," and
"G. M. Graham," the crew of the steamboat
on this trial voyage.[24] Howard, a friend of
Edwards from Denver, was said to have been

an old Lake Erie steamboat engineer and had come along to assist Edwards in getting the *Major Powell* in running order. Graham was reportedly a "health-seeker" from Montreal, Canada, and was probably along as a "paying guest."

A second round-trip by the steamer the following month was significant only in the fact that it resulted in the discovery of a second "D. Julien" inscription. In a 1908 letter to Robert Stanton, who at that time was compiling a history of the Colorado River, Edwards wrote, "It was on this trip that I first saw the inscription cut on the wall of Hell Roaring Canon . . . of 'D. Julien, 1836, 3 Mai.'"[25] This carving is still quite plain to see and is a popular stop for modern-day river runners descending the Green River. Taken together with another inscription located some nineteen miles farther upstream above

Bowknot Bend, but dated thirteen days later, historians and researchers have surmised that Julien may have been traveling upriver to that year's annual trapper and fur trader rendezvous at Horse Creek, on the upper Green River in southwestern Wyoming.

Use of the Green and Colorado as water routes for travel continued even after the ultimately futile effort to try to capitalize on the tourist trade. In the fall of 1896, George F. Flavell and a companion, Ramon Montez (some sources give the name as Montos), ran the length of the canyons from Green River, Wyoming, to Yuma, Arizona. Their stated intentions were to have adventure, to see the country, to hunt and trap, and to prospect for gold. A similar voyage in the winter of 1896–97 was made by Nathaniel Galloway and a companion, William C. Richmond, for much the same reasons.

Galloway, a native of Vernal, Utah, had been boating on the Green River for some six years and in 1895 had been down the Colorado as far as Lee's Ferry. His 1896–97 voyage with Richmond began at the foot of Flaming Gorge on the upper Green and ended at Needles, California, on the lower Colorado.[26] The lone inscription left from this trip is found in a small, shallow cave at the mouth of Royal Arch Creek in the Grand Canyon. It is written in charcoal and reads, "N. Galloway, Jan. 24, 1897," though his diary for that date makes no mention of its recording. Galloway continued his trapping and prospecting career on the Green and Colorado for over fifteen more years and even made another Grand Canyon traverse as a part of the Julius Stone expedition in 1909.

The rivers of the Colorado Plateau region never did develop into the transportation routes hoped. In their calm and placid stretches they were often too shallow, and in their rapid-studded canyons they were a barrier to any sort of large watercraft. As far as commercial traffic was concerned, they remained as little used as the rugged canyon and plateau country surrounding them.

SIXTEEN

FILLING IN THE CORNERS

1884–1899

By the decade of the 1890s, most of the Colorado Plateau region had been explored, and the inhabitable areas settled. Two of the last areas to be so utilized lie close together distance-wise, but are separated by the deep gorge of the Colorado River and the rapid-strewn length of Cataract Canyon. In the heart of today's Canyonlands National Park in southeastern Utah, the Green River and the Grand (prior to 1921) joined at a "Y" junction to form the Colorado. The sandstone-pinnacled plateau-land to the west came to be designated by the National Park Service as the Maze district, while the rock-spired area to the east was called the Needles district.

The region to the west is divided geographically into two areas: the higher, but canyoned, Land's End Plateau, and the lower, step-like flats known locally as Under the Ledge. Since at least the beginning of the 1880s, the Land's End Plateau was used by rustlers to hold stolen livestock. One of the first of these was "Cap" Brown, who rustled horses from the Mormon ranchers in western Utah and ultimately sold them in the mining towns of southwestern Colorado. By the mid-1880s and during much of the 1890s, other outlaw types drifted into and out of the area, giving the plateau its more commonly known name of Robbers Roost.

Collectively, the rather loose association of robbers, rustlers, and outlaws came to be called the Wild Bunch.

Undoubtedly the most famous of these men was Robert Leroy Parker, better known by his alias of Butch Cassidy. Adopting a self-styled Robin Hood–like image, he stole mainly from the large corporate-owned banks and railroads, supposedly never killed anyone until his later days in South America, and was said to be "generous" to the smaller settlers and townsfolk. There are four known Butch Cassidy inscriptions in southern Utah. Most, if not all, are probably spurious, but at least one of them may very well be authentic.

In the southern part of the San Rafael Swell region is an area known as Mussentuchit Flat. At the back of a shallow rock overhang, on one side of a normally dry wash, is "Butch Casady," printed in charcoal. While it does have the appearance of some age, the spelling of the last name makes it suspect. Also on the back wall of a shallow cave, this time along a natural waterway through the Capitol Reef cliffs, is incised "Butch Cassidy, 1884," the only one of the four inscriptions that also includes a date. In this case it is the date that gives evidence to the falseness of the signature. Though it is accepted among most researchers and historians that Robert

Parker did, in fact, make his first venture to Robbers Roost by way of the Capitol Reef area in 1884,[1] it was not until a few years later, in 1889,[2] that he seems to have taken on the sobriquet of "Butch Cassidy."

Along the bank of the Fremont River in Capitol Reef is the one-room stone cabin built by Elijah Behunin in 1892. The name "Butch Cassidy" was at one time cut into the back wall of the cabin. It was plastered over by the National Park Service in 1990 after a former maintenance employee testified to seeing an "unknown" man place the inscription there "sometime in the 1960s."[3] However, it must be noted that the story of Butch Cassidy himself carving his name there soon after the cabin was built has been handed down by descendants of Elijah Behunin for years. In fact, the story is printed in a biography of Elijah Behunin that was first published in 1961.[4]

The inscription that well may be authentic is carved into the rock wall of a shallow wash near Robbers Roost Spring. Written as "Butch Casidy," with only one "s," it is much more weathered and "older looking" in appearance than a carved date of 1912 just a couple of feet away on the same rock surface.

The first person to actually settle at the Roost was J. B. Buhr from Denver, Col-

orado, in 1890. He built a cabin just east of Robbers Roost Spring and, incredible as it may seem, stocked the range with fine horses. Many, if not most, of his riders were outlaws. In 1899 he finally took what few head of horses remained and left the country. By the latter part of the 1890s a few enterprising sheepmen began bringing their flocks to the grass-covered Land's End Plateau. There they would pasture them in the summer, taking them down to the lower benchlands of the Land of Standing Rocks and the Ernie Country in the winter.[5]

One inscription found in this area may possibly have been left by such a sheepman. Water on these winter benchlands was always a concern, and at one place a steep, rugged, but passable route led down another "level" lower to Spanish Bottom and the Colorado River. About a third of the way down, neatly carved into the rock, is "G. F. Laughter, 1896." The last name, Laughter, though unusual, is actually not uncommon on the Navajo Indian Reservation to the south. That tribe had long been noted for their herds of sheep, and so perhaps a Utah sheepman in the latter part of the 1890s hired a Navajo to help with his flock.

In the spring of 1897, following the holdup of the mine payroll at Castle Gate, Utah, Butch Cassidy and several members of

the so-called Wild Bunch hid out in the Robbers Roost area.[6] Some of them evidently stayed at a spring on what is known as Waterhole Flat. On a rock wall about 150 yards below the spring are some lightly scratched names, three with the year date of 1897. Two of these are "M. R. Butler" and "Ella Butler." Monte Butler was a rider for the 3-B outfit of J. B. Buhr up on the Land's End Plateau in the 1890s, but was also an occasional member of the Wild Bunch. Ella Butler was his wife. A raid by Grand County sheriff Jesse Tyler and posse in the spring of 1899 "wiped out" the last hangers-on of the outlaw element at Robbers Roost, but it would not be until 1909 that legitimate cattlemen made the Land's End Plateau area their permanent home.

On the eastern side of the Colorado River The Needles was also slow to attract anything like permanent settlement, and even then only on its eastern margin. The Needles area itself is a region of fault-created valleys, separated by blocks of bare sandstone that have been eroded into numerous columns and spires. Being formed by movements of the rocky crust rather than by running water, most of these valleys contain not even intermittent seasonal streams. Therefore water was, and always has been, at a premium.

Permanent settlement here has been in only one area: along the perennial stream of Indian Creek, flowing north from the Abajo Mountains. Where Cottonwood Creek comes in from the southwest, Mel Turner and David M. Cooper settled with a small herd of cattle in the fall of 1885. In the next couple of years several other small ranchers also came to Indian Creek.[7] Some of them grazed their cattle to the west in the Needles area during the winter months. In Chesler Park is an old cowboy camp with several inscriptions written on the sheltering sandstone wall. One of these, printed in charcoal, reads, "Bill Frawley, February 1887."

The area at the junction of Cottonwood and Indian Creeks was known as The Dugout, because when Turner and Cooper first came there that was the type of living quarters they built back into the hillside bordering the stream. Mel Turner stayed in the Needles region for several years,[8] and he perhaps scratched his name on the plastered wall of one of the rooms of the prehistoric site known as Whitewash Ruin just off of Horse Canyon. There are many names incised into the whitish mud-plastered wall, some crowding and almost overlapping others. One, however, appears to be "C. Melvin Turner," with a date of either "Feb. 1890" or "Jan. 1893."

Placerville, Co., M. R. Butler, Ella Butler 1897. Glen Canyon National Recreation Area, Utah.

Feb. 1890, C. Melvin. Canyonlands National Park, Utah.

Ed. Turner, Jan. 1893.
Canyonlands National
Park, Utah.

James Scorup, 1928.
Dry Valley, Utah.

Al, Jim. Canyonlands
National Park, Utah.

In the winter of 1891–92, brothers Al and Jim Scorup came from Salina, Utah, on the western side of the Colorado River, to run cattle in San Juan County. For the next several years they herded their stock, for the most part, on the north side of White Canyon. Then in 1898 they bought out the interests of the so-called Bluff Pool, a co-op of small Mormon stockmen from that San Juan River town. Now the two brothers extended their range farther north, from Elk Ridge to The Needles.[9] At an old cowboy camp at Cave Spring is a fading charcoal inscription perhaps left from this time, though all that can be made out now are the names "Al" and "Jim."

Later, in 1918, the Scorup brothers bought out the various owner-partners of the Indian Creek Cattle Company and established their headquarters at what was now called Dugout Ranch.[10] In the hollowed-out basin atop Sugar Loaf Rock, just a few miles east of Indian Creek at the edge of Dry Valley, many names are carved into the soft sandstone, including "James Scorup."

These last bastions of Colorado Plateau settlement, the Maze district on the west and the Needles district on the east, both now lie within the boundaries of Canyonlands National Park. However, the areas immediately bordering them remain rangeland for cattle even today. The Land's End Plateau area is now grazed by livestock from the Ekker family's Robbers Roost Ranch, while the Indian Creek area is ranged by cattle from the Redd family's Dugout Ranch.

SEVENTEEN

FULL CIRCLE

1909

As explained in the Preface, most of the historic inscriptions, names, and/or dates contained herein pre-date 1900. The exceptions, however, are covered in this chapter and represent a significant geographical discovery in the Colorado Plateau region. Somewhat ironically, but perhaps fittingly, these last inscriptions are found in the very region supposedly described in the purported Iberic inscription found at the southeastern corner of Navajo Mountain near the Utah-Arizona state line (see chapter 1).

In 1906, John and Louisa Wetherill established a trading post on the Navajo Indian Reservation at Ooljee'toh, or Oljato when it eventually received a post office. Stories eventually reached the post of a large natural bridge spanning a remote canyon somewhere on the northwest side of Navajo Mountain about thirty miles due west. It was said to be larger than any natural rock span then known, and reportedly only a few Navajo and Paiute Indians knew of its exact location. In the next year or so, two or three unsuccessful attempts were made to find the large bridge. Finally, at the end of the summer in 1909, a combined expedition from the University of Utah and the Government Land Office (now the Bureau of Land Management), led by John Wetherill, made its way to the natural bridge. The last part of

the journey, north of Navajo Mountain, they were guided by a local Paiute, Nasja Begay.

The rock span was named Rainbow Natural Bridge, from the Paiute word barohoini, meaning "rainbow." The name was suggestive of the curved, arching shape of the rock, in contrast to most natural bridges, which are relatively flat on top. The bridge was reached around midday on August 14, 1909. A member of the University of Utah archeological party, Neil M. Judd, in a book written many years later, said, "After we had rested a bit . . . Don Beauregard and John Wetherill found their way to the summit [the top of the natural bridge]. . . ."[1] It was probably at this time that Wetherill left his name and the date carved high above the bridge on this western side about halfway to the top of the mesa. Reading "J. Wetherill, Aug. 14, 1909," the inscription was first noted and photographed by Tad Nichols in August 1935.[2]

Just to the north of Rainbow Bridge and on the eastern side of the canyon is a short side gorge. A little way up it is a small, shallow alcove and on the back wall is carved, "John Wetherill, 8/14 1909." In the notebook of the trip kept by Professor Byron Cummings, head of the university group, he states, "Examined caves about the bridge. . . ."[3] Undoubtedly this was when Wetherill left this particular inscription.

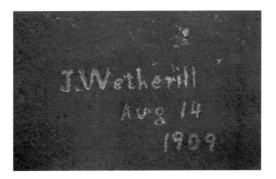

J. Wetherill,
Aug. 14, 1909.
Rainbow Bridge
National Monument,
Utah.

John Wetherill,
8/14 1909. Rainbow
Bridge National
Monument, Utah.

Later in the afternoon several members of the expedition followed down the canyon to the north to try to find where it joined the Colorado River. Some six miles later, about sundown, they reached their objective. They also found the prehistoric/historic rock structures near the mouth of the canyon and saw abandoned miners' tools and camp equipment, evidently left from the Glen Canyon gold rush. Donald Beauregard, one of the university students, in a newspaper article printed shortly after the archeological part of the expedition returned to Salt Lake City, said, "We found three names scratched with charcoal above the ruins. . . ."[4] Though he does not mention it, he also added his own signature to those already there, inscribing "Don Beauregard, 1909."

Fellow student Neil M. Judd, writing for the National Park Service in 1927, added, "Just within the mouth of Bridge [Forbidding] Canyon, under the overhanging north wall, is a dilapidated cliff-dwelling, reoccupied by later gold seekers."[5] Like Beauregard, Judd did not mention the fact in his article, but he too put his name with those in the alcove. Before the site was flooded by the rising waters of Lake Powell reservoir, his carving read, "N. M. Judd, 8/14/09."

In a magazine article written many years after the fact in 1940, Malcolm Cummings,

who as a youngster had accompanied his father on the Rainbow Bridge trip of 1909, related an interesting anecdote. On the morning of August 15, before the university party departed back for Oljato, one of the students, Stuart Young, began ". . . carving on the cliff wall below the arch in small letters . . ." a record of the discovery. But before he had gotten fairly started, William B. Douglass, head of the Government Land Office party, made stentorian objection, insisting that "This was to be a national monument, and marking on or defacing there was a misdemeanor, subject to fine and imprisonment."[6] Perhaps this explains why a third Wetherill inscription was placed, not on Rainbow Bridge itself, but on the inside surface of two leaning rock slabs under the eastern abutment of the arch, effectively hidden from view.

There is, however, one inscription that was carved on the bridge. Now weathered almost beyond seeing, photographs from the 1960s show it to read, "The Worlds Greatest Natural Bridge, 309 ft. High, 277 ft. Span, Discovered Aug. 14, 1909." After making their way back to Oljato, Douglass's government survey party returned to Rainbow Bridge about the first of October. They remeasured the rock span, arriving at the above figures.[7] Therefore, this inscription

 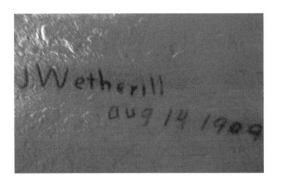

was probably cut into the inside of the eastern abutment by the Douglass party during this resurvey.

Today, almost a century later, Rainbow Bridge remains the largest natural bridge known in the world. Called the "Jewel of Lake Powell" by the National Park Service, which administers the surrounding Glen Canyon National Recreation Area, what was in 1909 arguably the most remote spot in the entire Colorado Plateau region is now visited by thousands of people each year, most of whom cruise up the lake on tourboats.

N. M. Judd, 8/14/09. Glen Canyon, Utah. Special Collections Dept., Marriott Library, University of Utah.

J. Wetherill, Aug. 14, 1909. Rainbow Bridge National Monument, Utah.

Afterword

BECAUSE THESE INSCRIPTIONS, ESPECIALLY the older ones, are a valuable part of the historic record, it is not only important, but absolutely essential that a written and photographic record be made of as many of them as is possible. For the simple fact is, they will not always be with us. Ultimately they will be erased by the natural processes of weathering and erosion. They also may be, and have been, destroyed by man-made works, such as roads, bridges, and reservoirs. And, unfortunately, some inscriptions have been, and will be, obliterated deliberately by other people.

In the past the National Park Service has been one of the principal culprits, albeit with good intentions, in the removal of historic inscriptions from various sites under their jurisdiction. This seemed to be especially true in the 1920s, when numbers of old names and dates were removed from the cliff dwellings comprising Navajo National Monument in northern Arizona and Mesa Verde National Park in southwestern Colorado. As government surveyor William B. Douglass so righteously intoned in 1909 at Rainbow Bridge, it is still today a federal misdemeanor to write on or in any way deface natural or made-made structures in any of the various units administered by the National Park Service. But at least they have backed off from the once-recognized practice of removing all inscriptions, old or new.

Of more concern at the present time are the growing numbers of environmentally sensitive people frequenting the newly established national monuments and wilderness areas of the Colorado Plateau region. In their fervor, they have obliterated and "erased" many old inscriptions dating back even into the 1800s. While it is now the commonly accepted practice not to carve or write modern names and dates on the canyon walls and rock boulders (though, unfortunately, some still do), care must be given to the well-meaning, but misguided, attempts to remove any historic inscriptions.

Be they names, dates, or sayings, these inscriptions are a link to us from the past. In many cases these signatures are the closest we will come to "speaking" with these now-deceased individuals. They tell us something of a time that has gone before, and as such, like any fact of history, they contribute to our knowledge of today.

Notes

CHAPTER ONE

1. Henriette Mertz, *Pale Ink*, photo facing p. 43.
2. Ibid., 146–56.
3. George C. Fraser, "Journal—1916," 137.
4. Stephen C. Jett, "An Alphabetical Inscription from Navajo Mountain, Arizona, and the Theories of Barry Fell," *Papers of the Archeological Society of New Mexico* 12 (1986): 19.

CHAPTER TWO

1. Hack Miller, "Julius F. Stone, Frazier to Re-run Part of Colorado," *The Deseret News* (September 20, 1938).
2. Katharine Bartlett and Harold S. Colton, "A Note on the Marcos de Niza Inscription Near Phoenix, Arizona," *Plateau* 12 (April 1940): 57.
3. George Parker Winship, ed., *The Journey of Coronado, 1540–1542*, 181.
4. Information, back of photo, *George Wharton James Photograph Collection*.
5. J. Donald Hughes, *In the House of Stone and Light*, 17–19.
6. C. Gregory Crampton, *Land of Living Rock*, 70.
7. Charles Kelly, "Colorado River Expedition, 1938," entry for "Thur. 29."
8. Harry L. Aleson, "Up-river Trip from Lee's Ferry, March 20–April 7, 1945," entry for "May 30 Wed."
9. Byron Cummings, *Indians I Have Known*, 25–26.
10. Albert E. Ward, *Inscription House*, 15–16.
11. George A. Thompson, *Lost Treasures on the Old Spanish Trail*, 39.
12. Gale R. Rhoades and Kerry Ross Boren, *Footprints in the Wilderness*, 333.
13. Richard Van Valkenburgh, "Inscription at Hwoye Spring," *Desert* 4 (January 1941): 9.
14. Austin Nelson Leiby, *Borderline Pathfinders*, 220.
15. Ted J. Warner, ed., *The Dominguez-Escalante Journal*, 53–54.
16. LeRoy R. Hafen, ed., "Armijo's Journal of 1829–30; the Beginning of Trade Between New Mexico and California," *The Colorado Magazine* 27 (April 1950): 122.
17. George C. Baldwin, "The Vanishing Inscription," *Journal of the Southwest* 41 (Summer 1999): 141.
18. Bert J. Silliman, "The Orejas del Oso Trail, or Bear's Ears Trail," no pagination.
19. Pearl Baker, "The Spanish Bottom Crossing of the Spanish Trail," 4.
20. LeRoy R. Hafen and Ann W. Hafen, *Old Spanish Trail*, 85–86.
21. Stella McElprang, ed., "*Castle Valley*," 14, 15, 16.

CHAPTER THREE

1. Richard Van Valkenburgh, *Navajo Country*, 81–82.
2. George R. Brooks, ed., *The Southwest Expedition of Jedediah S. Smith*, 58–59, n. 56.
3. Frank McNitt, ed., *Navaho Expedition*, 160–61.
4. Iris Higbee Wilson, *William Wolfskill, 1798–1866*, 73.
5. Charles Kelly, "Forgotten Trail of the Old West," *Desert* 13 (October 1950): 20–21.
6. Warren A. Ferris, *Life in the Rocky Mountains*, 353.
7. James H. Knipmeyer, "The Denis Julien In-

scriptions," *Utah Historical Quarterly* 64 (Winter 1996): 52–69.

8. Thomas Fitzpatrick to Milton Sublette, 13 November 1833. Letter.

9. C. Gregory Crampton, *Historical Sites in Glen Canyon, Mouth of Hansen Creek to Mouth of San Juan River*, 44, 45.

10. Charles Kelly, "Antoine Robidoux," *Utah Historical Quarterly* 6 (October 1933): 115–16.

11. Joseph Williams, *Narrative of a Tour . . . 1841–42*, 81.

12. Don Berry, *A Majority of Scoundrels*, 365–67.

CHAPTER FOUR

1. E. G. Beckwith, *Report of Explorations for a Route for the Pacific Railroad . . . 1853*, 69–71.

2. Joseph M. Bauman, Jr., *Stone House Lands*, 103–5.

3. Stella McElprang, ed., *"Castle Valley,"* 15.

4. Robert Shlaer, *Sights Once Seen*, 47–49.

5. Anne Snow, ed., *Rainbow Views*, 3.

6. L. R. Bailey, ed., *The Navajo Reconnaissance*, 84.

7. H. H. Sibley to L. L. Rich, 12 November 1860. Letter.

8. Frank McNitt, *Navajo Wars*, 401.

9. Raymond E. Lindgren, ed., "A Diary of Kit Carson's Navajo Campaign, 1863–1864," *New Mexico Historical Review* 21 (July 1946): 235.

10. Lawrence C. Kelly, ed., *Navajo Roundup*, 104.

11. Campbell Grant, *Canyon de Chelly*, 118.

CHAPTER FIVE

1. Donna T. Smart, "Over the Rim to Red Rock Country," *Utah Historical Quarterly* 62 (Spring 1994): 177–78.

2. H. Lorenzo Reid, *Dixie of the Desert*, 68.

3. Ibid., 92.

4. Janice F. De Mille, "Shonesburg: The Town Nobody Knows," *Utah Historical Quarterly* 45 (Winter 1977): 50.

5. Andrew Jensen, "The Elk Mountain Mission," *The Utah Genealogical and Historical Magazine* 4 (October 1913): 188–89.

6. William B. Pace, "Diary of William B. Pace During the Elk Mountain Mission, 1855–1856," 6.

7. Daniel W. Jones, *Forty Years Among the Indians*, 131.

8. John F. Hoffman, *Arches National Park*, 58.

9. Pearson H. Corbett, *Jacob Hamblin: The Peacemaker*, 67–68.

10. Ibid., 194–95.

11. Albert E. Ward, *Inscription House*, 9–10.

12. Ibid., 14.

13. Ibid.

14. Wesley P. Larsen, "Stories from House Rock Valley and Kaibab Plateau," 56.

15. C. Gregory Crampton, ed., "Military Reconnaissance in Southern Utah, 1866," *Utah Historical Quarterly* 32 (Spring 1964): 149.

16. Ibid., 152.

CHAPTER SIX

1. J. W. Powell, *Exploration of the Colorado River of the West . . .*, 71.

2. Frederick S. Dellenbaugh, *A Canyon Voyage*, 141.

3. Wesley P. Larsen, "The 'Letter,' or Were the Powell Men Really Killed by Indians?," *Canyon Legacy* 17 (Spring 1993): 12–19.

4. Michael Belshaw, "The Dunn-Howland Killings: A Reconstruction," *The Journal of Arizona History* 20 (Winter 1979): 416.

5. Wallace Stegner, *Beyond the Hundredth Meridian*, 135, 136.

6. Pearson H. Corbett, *Jacob Hamblin: The Peacemaker*, 299.

7. Herbert E. Gregory, ed., "Journal of Stephen Vandiver Jones, April 21, 1871–December 14, 1872," *Utah Historical Quarterly* 16–17 (1948–1949): 82.

8. Charles Kelly, ed., "Journal of W. C. Powell, April 21, 1871–December 7, 1872," *Utah Historical Quarterly* 16–17 (1948–1949): 340.

9. George H. Billingsley, et al., *Quest for the Pillar of Gold*, 50–51.

10. Edwin D. McKee, "Kanab Canyon: The Trail of Scientists," *Plateau* 18 (January 1946): 42.

11. Dellenbaugh, *A Canyon Voyage*, 20; Don D. Fowler, ed., *Photographed All the Best Scenery*, 125; "Diary of William D. Johnson, 1872," 1.

12. Fowler, *Photographed All the Best Scenery*, 125.

13. Dellenbaugh, *A Canyon Voyage*, 210.

14. William D. Johnson, "Diary of William D. Johnson," 10.

15. Otis Marston, "Those Names in the Cave," *Desert* 14 (June 1951): 23.

CHAPTER SEVEN

1. John M. Slater, *El Morro*, 25.

2. Wesley P. Larsen, "Stories from House Rock Valley . . .," 56.

3. Adonis Findlay Robinson, ed., *History of Kane County*, 523–24.

4. Michael A. Dussinger, "Signatures on Stone,"

no pagination.

5. Robert W. Olsen, Jr., "Pipe Spring, Arizona, and Thereabouts," *The Journal of Arizona History* 6 (Spring 1965): 19.

6. Margaret M. Verkamp, *History of Grand Canyon National Park*, 14.

7. George H. Billingsley, et al., *Quest for the Pillar of Gold*, 42.

8. Ibid., 64, 65.

9. "Up From Colorado Canon," *The Denver Republican* (July 17, 1892).

10. Dove Menkes, personal communication, 9 June 1992.

11. Clarence E. Dutton, *Tertiary History of the Grand Canon District*, 181, 182.

12. Charles D. Walcott, "Report of Charles B. Walcott," in *Fourth Annual Report of the United States Geological Survey, 1882–'83*, 46.

13. Frank E. Casanova, ed., "General Crook Visits the Supais . . .," *Arizona and the West* 10 (Autumn 1968): 272.

14. Edward A. Mearns, "Field Notes," no pagination.

15. Michael F. Anderson, *Living at the Edge*, 70.

CHAPTER EIGHT

1. Adonis Findlay Robinson, ed., *History of Kane County*, 20.

2. Ibid., 486–87.

3. Arthur F. Bruhn, *Exploring Southern Utah's Land of Color*, 71.

4. Stan Jones, *Ramblings By Boat and Boot*, 146.

5. John W. Van Cott, *Utah Place Names*, 2.

6. Nethella Griffin Woolsey, *The Escalante Story*, 127, 128.

7. Miriam B. Murphy, *A History of Wayne County*, 137.

8. Rose Houk, *Capitol Reef*, 13.

9. Bradford J. Frye, *From Barrier to Crossroads*, 50.

10. Sidney Hanks and Ephraim K. Hanks, *Scouting for the Mormons on the Great Frontier*, 228.

11. Anne Snow, *Rainbow Views*, 293, 294.

12. Kerry William Bate, *The Ebenezer Hanks Story*, 208.

13. Edward A. Geary, *A History of Emery County*, 50.

14. Reed Martin, personal communication, 10 May 2000.

CHAPTER NINE

1. Robert Glass Cleland and Juanita Brooks, eds., *A Mormon Chronicle* II, 180.

2. Ibid., 185.

3. Frederick S. Dellenbaugh, *A Canyon Voyage*, 160.

4. "Minutes," *The Deseret News* (May 28, 1873).

5. Cleland and Brooks, eds., *A Mormon Chronicle* II, 245.

6. James H. McClintock, *Mormon Settlement in Arizona*, 86–87.

7. John H. Standifird, "Journal of John Henry Standifird, Vol. I," 21.

8. Ibid., 22.

9. Ibid., 26.

10. William H. Solomon, "Arizona Mission," 19.

11. Ibid., 21.

12. Grand Canyon Pioneers Society, "House Rock Springs, Arizona: Survey of Inscriptions, April 25–26, 1992," 1.

13. Ted J. Warner, ed., *The Dominguez-Escalante Journal*, 110–11.

14. McClintock, *Mormon Settlement in Arizona*, 138.

15. Mildred and C. R. Hooper, "The Lore of Houserock Valley," *Outdoor Arizona* 49 (August 1977): 18.

16. Mildred and C. R. Hooper, "Travel the Honeymoon Trail," *Outdoor Arizona* 48 (May 1976): 17.

CHAPTER TEN

1. Frank Hall, *A History of the State of Colorado*, vol. 4, 167.

2. Hall, *A History of the State of Colorado*, vol. 2, 199, 201.

3. Herbert E. Gregory and Raymond C. Moore, *The Kaiparowits Region*, 147.

4. Robert Glass Cleland and Juanita Brooks, eds., *A Mormon Chronicle* II, 270, 272.

5. Ibid., 243, 244, 272, 302, 309, 311, 312, 313, 327, 334.

6. William H. Jackson, *The Diaries of William Henry Jackson: Frontier Photographer*, 309–10.

7. W. H. Holmes, "Report on the Ruins of Southwestern Colorado . . . 1875 and 1876," in S. V. Hayden, *Tenth Annual Report of the U.S. Geological and Geographical Survey of the Territories*, 397.

8. William H. Jackson, *Time Exposure*, 258.

9. William H. Jackson, "Diary—1875," entry for "Aug. 4th."

10. Robert J. Bruns, "The First We Know," 54.

11. Cornelia Adams Perkins, et al., *Sage of San Juan*, 89.

12. Charles S. Peterson, *Look to the Mountains*, 91.

13. Faun McConkie Tanner, *The Far Country*, 177.

CHAPTER ELEVEN

1. "Camp Records," in "San Juan Stake History," entry for April 23.

2. Ibid., entries for May 3–7.

3. Ibid., entry for April 25.

4. David E. Miller, *Hole-in-the-Rock*, 143.

5. Ibid., 144.

6. Ibid., 89.

7. Ibid., 98.

8. Ibid., 122, 123.

9. C. Gregory Crampton, *Historical Sites in Glen Canyon, Mouth of Hansen Creek to Mouth of San Juan River*, 13–14.

10. Miller, *Hole-in-the-Rock*, 168.

11. Ibid., 134.

12. Ibid.

13. Ibid., 137.

14. Charles Redd, "Short Cut to San Juan," *1949 Brand Book*, 23–24.

15. Miller, *Hole-in-the-Rock*, 140.

16. Cornelia Adams Perkins, et al., *Saga of San Juan*, 331.

CHAPTER TWELVE

1. Faun McConkie Tanner, *The Far Country*, 76.

2. Ibid.

3. Richard A. Firmage, *A History of Grand County*, 111.

4. Samuel Taylor, personal communication, 18 September 1986.

5. Charles S. Peterson, *Look to the Mountains*, 86.

6. Phyllis Cortes, ed., *Grand Memories*, 270.

7. J. T. Farrer, Sr., *Life in the Middle West*, 18.

8. Ibid., 18, 19.

9. Gordon Chappell, *Scenic Line of the World*, 66.

CHAPTER THIRTEEN

1. William Haas Moore, *Chiefs, Agents and Soldiers*, 223.

2. Gladwell Richardson, *Navajo Trader*, 94.

3. Frances Gillmor and Louisa Wade Wetherill, *Traders to the Navajos*, 17.

4. Galen Eastman to Commissioner of Indian Affairs, 4 August 1882. Letter.

5. Martin Clark Powell, "A Study and Historical Analysis of the Document 'The Trail of Hosteen Pish La Ki for Sixty Snows,'" 20–21.

6. "Gone to the Navajo Mountain," *The Durango Record* (January 18, 1882).

7. "Nothing of Note Comes from Navajo Mountain," *Rocky Mountain News* (April 13, 1882).

8. "Gone to the Navajo Mountain."

9. Ibid.

10. "Nothing of Note Comes from Navajo Mountain."

11. "Another Song Sung by Navajo Explorers," *Rocky Mountain News* (April 14, 1882).

12. Ibid.

13. "A Prospecting Party Goes to Monumental Valley," *Rocky Mountain News* (May 23, 1882).

14. Richardson, *Navajo Trader*, 94.

15. "A Prospecting Party Goes to Monumental Valley."

16. Pearl Baker, *Trail on the Water*, 63–64.

17. Ibid., 64.

18. Laura C. Clark, *An Enduring Symbol of Pioneer Vision*, 112.

19. Ibid.

20. "Big Stampede to Utah," *Salt Lake Herald* (December 13, 1892).

21. "A. Koebler Returns," *The Durango Daily Herald* (January 11, 1893).

22. C. Gregory Crampton, *The San Juan Canyon Historic Sites*, 18.

CHAPTER FOURTEEN

1. Frank McNitt, *Richard Wetherill: Anasazi*, 23–25.

2. Ibid., 27.

3. Ibid., 30.

4. Alden C. Hayes, *The Archeological Survey of Wetherill Mesa*, 33.

5. McNitt, *Richard Wetherill: Anasazi*, 3.

6. Fred M. Blackburn and Ray A. Williamson, *Cowboys & Cave Dwellers*, 4–5.

7. Helen Sloan Daniels, "Charles Cary Graham's Explorations," *Adventures With the Anasazi of Falls Creek*, 10.

8. Ibid., 15.

9. Charlie R. Steen, "The Natural Bridges of White Canyon: A Diary of H. L. A. Culmer, 1905," *Utah Historical Quarterly* 40 (Winter 1972): 75.

10. Warren K. Moorehead, "In Search of a Lost Race," *The Illustrated American* (July 23, 1892): 460.

11. Warren K. Moorehead, "In Search of a Lost Race," *The Illustrated American* (July 30, 1892): 512.

12. Warren K. Moorehead, "Field Diary of an Archeological Collector," 30–31.

13. Lewis W. Gunckel, "In Search of a Lost Race," *The Illustrated American* (August 6, 1892): 559.

14. Ibid., 562.

15. Fred M. Blackburn and Victoria M. Atkins, "Handwriting on the Wall: Applying Inscriptions to Reconstruct Historic Archeological Expeditions," in Victoria M. Atkins, ed., *Anasazi Basketmaker*, 69–87.

16. Ann Phillips, "Archeological Expeditions into Southeastern Utah and Southwestern Colorado Between 1888–1898," in Victoria M. Atkins, ed., *Anasazi Basketmaker*, 113.

17. John Wetherill, "Navajo National Monument," *Southwestern Monuments Monthly Report* (March 1934): 2.

18. Alfred Vincent Kidder and Samuel J. Guernsey, *Archeological Explorations in Northeastern Arizona*, 92.

19. Blackburn and Atkins, "Handwriting on the Wall," 87–100.

20. McNitt, *Richard Wetherill: Anasazi*, 160.

21. Charles L. Bernheimer, "Field Notes—C. L. Bernheimer Expedition, 1924," 24.

22. David A. Breternitz, *Archeological Investigations in Turkey Cave (NA2520), Navajo National Monument, 1963*, 7.

CHAPTER FIFTEEN

1. Arthur A. Baker, *Geology of the Monument Valley–Navajo Mountain Region, San Juan County, Utah*, 88.

2. Helen J. Stiles, ed., "Down the Colorado in 1889," *The Colorado Magazine* 41 (Summer 1964): 239.

3. Allen Nossaman, personal communication, 18 August 1993.

4. Stiles, "Down the Colorado in 1889," 240.

5. Dwight L. Smith and C. Gregory Crampton, eds., *The Colorado River Survey*, 36.

6. James H. Knipmeyer, "Denis Julien: Midwestern Fur Trader," *Missouri Historical Review* 95 (April 2001): 246, 263.

7. Dwight L. Smith, ed., *Down the Colorado: Robert Brewster Stanton*, 71–72.

8. Dwight L. Smith, ed., *The Photographer and the River, 1889–90*, 39.

9. Smith and Crampton, *The Colorado River Survey*, 81.

10. William H. Edwards, "Diary of William H. Edwards, Boatman on the D.C.C. & P.R.R. Survey of 1889 & '90," 6.

11. Ibid., 10.

12. Smith and Crampton, *The Colorado River Survey*, 139.

13. Edwards, "Diary," 17.

14. Leo G. Brown, "Diary of L. G. Brown, 1889–1890," 7.

15. Robert Sorgenfrei, "'A Fortune Awaits Enterprise Here': The Best Mining Expedition to the Grand Canyon in 1891," *Journal of the Southwest* 40 (Winter 1998): 454.

16. William H. Edwards, "The Best Expedition, 1891," 8.

17. Sorgenfrei, "A Fortune Awaits Enterprise Here . . .," 457.

18. Ibid., 458.

19. J. A. McCormick, "The Colorado Grand Canon Mining & Improvement Company Expedition of 1891," 26.

20. Jim Knipmeyer, "The F. G. Faatz Inscriptions," *The Confluence* 6 (Winter 1999): 20–21.

21. Jim Knipmeyer, "The G. M. Wright Inscriptions," *The Confluence* 22 (February 2001): 19–20.

22. P. T. Reilly, *Lee's Ferry*, 134–38.

23. Richard E. Lingenfelter, *Steamboats on the Colorado River, 1852–1916*, 109.

24. C. Gregory Crampton, *Historical Sites in Cataract and Narrow Canyons, and in Glen Canyon to California Bar*, 6–7.

25. Robert B. Stanton, "Steamboat Navigation," in "The River and the Canyon," no pagination.

26. David Lavender, *River Runners of the Grand Canyon*, 36–38.

CHAPTER SIXTEEN

1. Pearl Baker, *The Wild Bunch at Robbers Roost*, 17, 19.

2. Richard Patterson, *Butch Cassidy: A Biography*, 56–57.

3. Norman R. Henderson, personal communication, 2 June 1993.

4. Ruby Noyes Tippets, *A Song in Her Heart*, 112.

5. Pearl Baker, *Robbers Roost Recollections*, 33.

6. Charles Kelly, *The Outlaw Trail*, 159.

7. Cornelia Adams Perkins, et al., *Saga of San Juan*, 192.

8. Charles S. Peterson, *Look to the Mountains*, 167.

9. C. Gregory Crampton, *Standing Up Country*, 116.

10. Stena Scorup, *J. A. Scorup: A Utah Cattleman*, 41.

CHAPTER SEVENTEEN

1. Neil M. Judd, *Men Met Along the Trail*, 42.

2. Otis H. Chidester, "The Discovery of Rainbow Bridge," *The Smoke Signal* 20 (Fall 1969): 218, 219.

3. Byron Cummings, "Field Notebook No. 3," no pagination.

4. Donald Beauregard, "'Nonnezhozhi,' the Father of All Natural Bridges," *Deseret Evening News* (October 2, 1909).

5. Neil Merton Judd, "The Discovery of Rainbow Bridge," *National Parks Bulletin* 54 (November 1927): 15.

6. Malcolm Cummings, "I Finished Last in the Race to Rainbow Bridge," *Desert* 3 (May 1940): 25.

7. William B. Douglass to Commissioner of General Land Office, 29 October 1909. Letter.

Bibliography

"A. Koebler Returns," *The Durango Daily Herald* (January 11, 1893).

Aleson, Harry L. "Up-river Trip from Lee's Ferry, March 20–April 7, 1945." Aleson Collection. Utah State Historical Society, Salt Lake City.

Anderson, Michael F. *Living at the Edge: Explorers, Exploiters and Settlers of the Grand Canyon Region.* Grand Canyon, Arizona: Grand Canyon Association, 1998.

"Another Song Sung by Navajo Explorers," *Rocky Mountain News* (April 14, 1882).

Atkins, Victoria M., ed. *Anasazi Basketmaker: Papers from the 1990 Wetherill–Grand Gulch Symposium.* Cultural Resources Series No. 24. Salt Lake City, Utah: Bureau of Land Management, 1993.

Aton, James M., and Robert S. McPherson. *River Flowing from the Sunrise: An Environmental History of the Lower San Juan.* Logan, Utah: Utah State University Press, 2000.

Bailey, L. R., ed. *The Navajo Reconnaissance: A Military Exploration of the Navajo Country in 1859.* Los Angeles: Westernlore Press, 1964.

Baker, Arthur A. *Geology of the Monument Valley–Navajo Mountain Region, San Juan County, Utah.* Geological Survey Bulletin 865. Washington: U.S. Government Printing Office, 1936.

Baker, Pearl. *Robbers Roost Recollections.* Logan, Utah: Utah State University Press, 1976.

———. "The Spanish Bottom Crossing of the Spanish Trail." Gift copy in possession of author.

———. *Trail on the Water.* Boulder, Colorado: Pruett Publishing Company, no date.

———. *The Wild Bunch at Robbers Roost.* New York: Abelard-Schuman, 1971.

Baldwin, George C. "The Vanishing Inscription," *Journal of the Southwest* 41 (Summer 1999): 119–76.

Bartlett, Katharine, and Harold S. Colton. "A Note on the Marcos de Niza Inscription near Phoenix, Arizona," *Plateau* 12 (April 1940): 53–59.

Bartlett, Richard A. *Great Surveys of the American West.* Norman: University of Oklahoma Press, 1962.

Bate, Kerry William. *The Ebenezer Hanks Story.* Provo, Utah: M. C. Printing, 1982.

Bauman, Jr., Joseph M. *Stone House Lands: The San Rafael Reef.* Salt Lake City: University of Utah Press, 1987.

Beauregard, Donald. "'Nonnezhozhi,' the Father of All Natural Bridges," *Deseret Evening News* (October 2, 1909).

Beckwith, E. G. *Report of Explorations for a Route for the Pacific Railroad by Capt. J. W. Gunnison, Topographical Engineers, near the 38th and 39th Parallels of North Latitude, From the Mouth of the Kansas River, Mo. to the Sevier Lake, in the Great Basin.* Washington: A. O. P. Nicholson, Printer, 1855.

Belshaw, Michael. "The Dunn-Howland Killings: A Reconstruction," *The Journal of Arizona History* 20 (Winter 1979): 409–22.

Bernheimer, Charles L. "Field Notes—C. L. Bernheimer Expedition, 1924." Files. Utah State Historical Society, Salt Lake City.

Berry, Don. *A Majority of Scoundrels: An Informal History of the Rocky Mountain Fur Company.* New York: Harper and Brothers, 1961.

"Big Stampede to Utah," *Salt Lake Herald* (December 13, 1892).

Billingsley, George H., Earl E. Spamer, and Dove Menkes. *Quest for the Pillar of Gold: The Mines and Miners of the Grand Canyon.* Monograph No. 10. Grand Canyon, Arizona: Grand Canyon Association, 1997.

Blackburn, Fred M., and Victoria M. Atkins. "Handwriting on the Wall: Applying Inscriptions to Reconstruct Historic Archeological Expeditions." In *Anasazi Basketmaker: Papers from the 1990 Wetherill–Grand Gulch Symposium,* edited by Victoria M. Atkins. Cultural Resources Series No. 24. Salt Lake City, Utah: Bureau of Land Management, 1993.

Blackburn, Fred M., and Ray A. Williamson. *Cowboys & Cave Dwellers: Basketmaker Archeology in Utah's Grand Gulch.* Santa Fe, New Mexico: School of American Research Press, 1997.

Bolton, Herbert E., ed. *Pageant in the Wilderness: The Story of the Escalante Expedition to the Interior Basin, 1776.* Salt Lake City: Utah State Historical Society, 1950.

Bradley, Martha Sonntag. *A History of Kane County.* Salt Lake City: Utah State Historical Society, 1999.

Breternitz, David A. *Archeological Investigations in Turkey Cave (NA2520), Navajo National Monument, 1963.* Technical Series No. 8. Flagstaff, Arizona: Museum of Northern Arizona, 1969.

Brooks, George R., ed. *The Southwest Expedition of Jedediah S. Smith: His Personal Account of the Journey to California, 1826–1827.* Glendale, California: The Arthur H. Clark Company, 1977.

Brooks, Juanita. *John Doyle Lee: Zealot, Pioneer Builder, Scapegoat.* Glendale, California: The Arthur H. Clark Company, 1972.

Brown, Leo G. "Diary of L. G. Brown, 1889–1890." Otis R. Marston Collection. The Huntington Library, San Marino, California.

Bruhn, Arthur F. *Exploring Southern Utah's Land of Color.* Springdale, Utah: Zion Natural History Association, 1993.

Bruns, Robert J. "The First We Know: The Pioneer History of the San Juan." 1898. Files. San Juan County Historical Society, Silverton, Colorado.

"Camp Records," in "San Juan Stake History." 1879. Files. L.D.S. Church Historian's Library, Salt Lake City, Utah.

Casanova, Frank E., ed. "General Crook Visits the Supais: As Reported by John C. Bourke," *Arizona and the West* 10 (Autumn 1968): 253–76.

Chappell, Gordon. *Scenic Line of the World: The Story of America's Only Narrow Gauge Transcontinental.* Golden, Colorado: Colorado Railroad Historical Foundation, 1977.

Chidester, Ida, and Eleanor Bruhn, eds. *"Golden Nuggets of Pioneer Days": A History of Garfield County.* Panguitch, Utah: The Garfield County News, 1949.

Chidester, Otis H. "The Discovery of Rainbow Bridge," *The Smoke Signal* 20 (Fall 1969): 210–30.

Clark, Laura Christensen. *An Enduring Symbol of Pioneer Vision.* Privately printed, no date.

Cleland, Robert Glass. *This Reckless Breed of Men: The Trappers and Fur Traders of the Southwest.* New York: Alfred A. Knopf, 1963.

Cleland, Robert Glass, and Juanita Brooks, eds. *A Mormon Chronicle: The Diaries of John D. Lee, 1848–1876.* 2 volumes. Salt Lake City, Utah: University of Utah Press, 1983.

Corbett, Pearson H. *Jacob Hamblin: The Peacemaker.* Salt Lake City: Deseret Book Company, 1952.

Cortes, Phyllis, ed. *"Grand Memories."* Salt Lake City: Daughters of Utah Pioneers, Grand County, Utah, 1972.

Crampton, C. Gregory. *Historical Sites in Cataract and Narrow Canyons, and in Glen Canyon to California Bar.* Anthropological Paper No. 72. Salt Lake City: University of Utah Press, 1964.

———. *Historical Sites in Glen Canyon, Mouth of Hansen Creek to Mouth of San Juan River.* Anthropological Paper Number 61. Salt Lake City: University of Utah Press, 1962.

———. *Land of Living Rock: The Grand Canyon and the High Plateaus of Arizona, Utah, Nevada.* New York: Alfred A. Knopf, 1972.

———. *Outline History of the Glen Canyon Region, 1776-1922.* Anthropological Paper No. 42. Salt Lake City: University of Utah Press, 1959.

———. *The San Juan Canyon Historical Sites.* Anthropological Paper No. 70. Salt Lake City: University of Utah Press, 1964.

———. *Standing Up Country: The Canyonlands of Utah and Arizona.* New York: Alfred A. Knopf, 1964.

Crampton, C. Gregory, ed. "Military Reconnaissance in Southern Utah, 1866," *Utah Historical Quarterly* 32 (Spring 1964): 145–61.

Cummings, Byron. "Field Notebook No. 3." 1909. Papers of Byron Cummings. Arizona State Museum, Tucson.

———. *Indians I Have Known.* Tucson, Arizona: Arizona Silhouettes, 1952.

Cummings, Malcolm. "I Finished Last in the Race to Rainbow Bridge," *Desert* 3 (May 1940): 22–25.

Daniels, Helen Sloan. *Adventures With the Anasazi of Falls Creek.* Occasional Papers No. 3. Durango, Colorado: Center of Southwestern Studies, 1976.

Dellenbaugh, Frederick S. *A Canyon Voyage: The Narrative of the Second Powell Expedition down the Green-Colorado River from Wyoming, and the Explorations on Land, in the Years 1871 and 1872.* New Haven: Yale University Press, 1962.

———. *The Romance of the Colorado River: The Story of Its Discovery in 1540, with an Account of the Later Explorations, and with Special Reference to the Voyages of Powell through the Line of the Great Canyons.* Chicago, Illinois: The Rio Grande Press, 1965.

De Mille, Janice F. "Shonesburg: The Town Nobody Knows," *Utah Historical Quarterly* 45 (Winter 1977): 47-60.

Denver Posse of The Westerners. *The 1949 Brand Book.* Fifth Annual Volume. Boulder, Colorado: Johnson Publishing Company, 1950.

Douglass, William B. "Douglass to Commissioner of General Land Office, 29 October 1909."

Rainbow Bridge National Monument Collection. Northern Arizona University Library, Flagstaff.

Dussinger, Michael A. "Signatures on Stone: Historic Inscriptions of the North Kaibab Ranger District, Kaibab National Forest, Arizona." 1996. Files. North Kaibab Ranger District Offices, Fredonia, Arizona.

Dutton, Clarence E. *Tertiary History of the Grand Canon District*. Santa Barbara and Salt Lake City: Peregrine Smith, Inc., 1977.

Eastman, Galen. "Eastman to Commissioner of Indian Affairs, 4 August 1882." Record Group 75. National Archives and Records Service, Washington, D. C.

Edwards, William H. "The Best Expedition, 1891." Robert B. Stanton Papers. New York Public Library.

———. "The Diary of William H. Edwards: Boatman on the D.C.C. & P.R.R. Survey of 1889 & '90." Otis R. Marston Collection. The Huntington Library, San Marino, California.

Farrer, Sr., J. T. *Life in the Middle West*. Cloverdale, California: Laurelwood Publishing and Printing, no date.

Ferris, Warren A. *Life in the Rocky Mountains: A Diary of Wanderings on the Sources of the Rivers Missouri, Columbia, and Colorado, 1830–1835*. Denver, Colorado: Old West Publishing Company, 1983.

Firmage, Richard A. *A History of Grand County*. Salt Lake City: Utah State Historical Society, 1996.

Fitzpatrick, Thomas. "Fitzpatrick to Milton Sublette, 13 November 1833." Letter, Sublette Collection. Missouri Historical Society, St. Louis.

Fletcher, Maurine S. *The Wetherills of the Mesa Verde: Autobiography of Benjamin Alfred Wetherill*. Cranbury, New Jersey: Association of University Presses, Inc., 1977.

Fowler, Don D., ed. *"Photographed All the Best Scenery": Jack Hillers' Diary of the Powell Expeditions, 1871–1875*. Salt Lake City, Utah: University of Utah Press, 1972.

Fraser, George C. "Journal—1916." Fraser Collection. Princeton University Library, Princeton, New Jersey.

Freeman, Ira S., ed. *A History of Montezuma County, Colorado*. Boulder, Colorado: Johnson Publishing Company, 1958.

Frye, Bradford J. *From Barrier to Crossroads: An Administrative History of Capitol Reef National Park, Utah*. 2 volumes. Cultural Resources Selections No. 12. Denver, Colorado: National Park Service, 1998.

Geary, Edward A. *A History of Emery County*. Salt Lake City: Utah State Historical Society, 1996.

———. *The Proper Edge of the Sky: The High Plateau Country of Utah*. Salt Lake City: University of Utah Press, 1992.

Gillmor, Frances, and Louisa Wade Wetherill. *Traders to the Navajos: The Story of the Wetherills of Kayenta*. Albuquerque: University of New Mexico Press, 1952.

Goetzmann, William H. *Army Exploration in the American West, 1803–1863*. Austin: Texas State Historical Association, 1991.

———. *Exploration and Empire: The Explorer and the Scientist in the Winning of the Ameri-*

can West. Austin: Texas State Historical Association, 1993.

"Gone to the Navajo Mountain," *The Durango Record* (January 18, 1882).

Grand Canyon Pioneers Society. "House Rock Springs, Arizona: Survey of Inscriptions, April 25–26, 1992." Files. Grand Canyon Pioneers Society, Flagstaff, Arizona.

Grant, Campbell. *Canyon de Chelly: Its People and Rock Art.* Tucson, Arizona: University of Arizona Press, 1978.

Gregory, Herbert E., and Raymond C. Moore. *The Kaiparowits Region: A Geographical and Geological Reconnaissance of Parts of Utah and Arizona.* Geological Survey Professional Paper 164. Washington: U.S. Government Printing Office, 1931.

Gregory, Herbert E., ed. "Diary of Almon Harris Thompson." *Utah Historical Quarterly* 7 (January, April, and July 1939): 2–140.

———. "Journal of Stephen Vandiver Jones, April 21 1871–December 14, 1872," *Utah Historical Quarterly* 16–17 (1948–1949): 19–174.

Gunckel, Lewis W. "In Search of a Lost Race," *The Illustrated American* (August 6, 1892): 559–63.

Hafen, LeRoy R., and Ann W. Hafen. *Old Spanish Trail: Santa Fe to Los Angeles.* Glendale, California: The Arthur H. Clark Company, 1954.

Hafen, LeRoy R., ed. "Armijo's Journal of 1829–30; the Beginning of Trade Between New Mexico and California," *The Colorado Magazine* 27 (April 1950): 120–31.

Hall, Frank. *A History of the State of Colorado.* 4 volumes. Chicago: The Blakely Printing Company, 1885–95.

Hanks, Sidney, and Ephraim K. Hanks. *Scouting for the Mormons on the Great Frontier.* Salt Lake City: Deseret Book Company, 1948.

Hassell, Hank. *Rainbow Bridge: An Illustrated History.* Logan, Utah: Utah State University Press, 1999.

Hayden, S. V. *Tenth Annual Report of the U. S. Geological and Geographical Survey of the Territories in 1876.* Washington: U.S. Government Printing Office, 1878.

Hayes, Alden C. *The Archeological Survey of Wetherill Mesa, Mesa Verde National Park, Colorado.* Archeological Research Series No. 7-A. Washington, D. C.: Government Printing Office, 1964.

Henderson, Norman R. Personal communication, 2 June 1993.

Hoffman, John F. *Arches National Park: An Illustrated Guide and History.* San Diego, California: Western Recreational Publications, 1985.

Holmes, W. H. "Report on the Ancient Ruins of Southwestern Colorado, Examined During the Summers of 1875 and 1876." In *Tenth Annual Report of the U. S. Geological and Geographical Survey of the Territories in 1876,* by S. V. Hayden. Washington: U.S. Government Printing Office, 1878.

Hooper, Mildred, and C. R. Hooper. "The Lore of Houserock Valley," *Outdoor Arizona* 49 (August 1977): 16–19.

———. "Travel the Honeymoon Trail," *Outdoor Arizona* 48 (May 1976): 15–18.

Houk, Rose. *Capitol Reef: Canyon Country Eden.* Torrey, Utah: Capitol Reef Natural History Association, 1996.

Hughes, J. Donald. *In the House of Stone and*

Light: A Human History of the Grand Canyon. Grand Canyon, Arizona: Grand Canyon Natural History Association, 1978.

Hunt, Charles B. *Geology and Geography of the Henry Mountains Region, Utah.* Geological Survey Professional Paper 228. Washington: U.S. Government Printing Office, 1953.

Hunt, Charles B., ed. *Geology of the Henry Mountains, Utah, as recorded in the notebooks of G. K. Gilbert, 1875–76.* Memoir 167. Boulder, Colorado: The Geological Society of America, 1988.

Jackson, William H. *The Diaries of William Henry Jackson: Frontier Photographer.* Glendale, California: The Arthur H. Clark Company, 1959.

———. "Diary—1875." Files. Colorado Historical Society, Denver.

———. *Time Exposure: The Autobiography of William Henry Jackson.* New York: G. P. Putnam and Company, 1940.

Jacobs, G. Clell. "The Phantom Pathfinder: Juan Maria Antonio de Rivera and his Expedition." *Utah Historical Quarterly* 60 (Summer 1992): 200–23.

Jensen, Andrew. "The Elk Mountain Mission," *The Utah Genealogical and Historical Magazine* 4 (October 1913): 188–200.

Jett, Stephen C. "An Alphabetical Inscription from Navajo Mountain, Arizona, and the Theories of Barry Fell." *By Hands Unknown: Papers on Rock Art and Archeology in Honor of James G. Bain.* Papers of the Archeological Society of New Mexico No. 12. Santa Fe: Ancient City Press, Inc., 1986.

———. "The Great 'Race' to 'Discover' Rainbow Natural Bridge in 1909." *Kiva* 58 (Number 1, 1992): 3–66.

Johnson, William D. "Diary of William D. Johnson, 1872." Harry Aleson Collection. Utah State Historical Society, Salt Lake City.

Jones, Daniel W. *Forty Years Among the Indians: A True Yet Thrilling Narrative of the Author's Experiences Among the Natives.* Los Angeles: Westernlore Press, 1960.

Jones, Stan. *Ramblings by Boat and Boot in Lake Powell Country.* Page, Arizona: Sun Country Publications, 1998.

Judd, Neil M. *Men Met Along the Trail.* Norman: University of Oklahoma Press, 1968.

Judd, Neil Merton. "The Discovery of Rainbow Bridge," *National Parks Bulletin* 54 (November 1927): 6–16.

Kelly, Charles. "Antoine Robidoux," *Utah Historical Quarterly* 6 (October 1933): 115–16.

———. "Colorado River Expedition, 1938." Kelly Collection. Utah State Historical Society, Salt Lake City.

———. "Forgotten Trail of the Old West," *Desert* 13 (October 1959): 19–22.

———. *The Outlaw Trail: A History of Butch Cassidy and His Wild Bunch.* New York: Bonanza Books, 1959.

Kelly, Charles, ed. "Journal of W. C. Powell, April 21, 1871–December 7, 1872," *Utah Historical Quarterly* 16–17 (1948–1949): 257–478.

Kelly, Lawrence C., ed. *Navajo Roundup: Selected Correspondence of Kit Carson's Expedition Against the Navajo, 1863–1865.* Boulder, Colorado: The Pruett Publishing Company, 1970.

Kidder, Alfred Vincent, and Samuel J. Guernsey. *Archeological Investigations in Northeastern Arizona.* Bureau of American Ethnology Bulletin 65. Washington: U.S. Government Printing Office, 1919.

Knipmeyer, James H. "Denis Julien: Midwestern Fur Trader," *Missouri Historical Review* 95 (April 2001): 245–63.

Knipmeyer, James H. "The Denis Julien Inscriptions," *Utah Historical Quarterly* 64 (Winter 1996): 52–69.

Knipmeyer, Jim. "The F. G. Faatz Inscriptions," *The Confluence* 6 (Winter 1999): 20–21.

Knipmeyer, Jim. "The G. M. Wright Inscriptions," *The Confluence* 22 (February 2001): 19–20.

Larsen, Wesley P. "The 'Letter,' or Were the Powell Men Really Killed by Indians?" *Canyon Legacy* 17 (Spring 1993): 12–19.

Larsen, Wesley P. *Stories from House Rock Valley and Kaibab Plateau.* Privately printed, no date.

Lavender, David. *Colorado River Country.* New York: E. P. Dutton, Inc., 1982.

Lavender, David. *River Runners of the Grand Canyon.* Tucson, Arizona: University of Arizona Press, 1985.

Leiby, Austin Nelson. *Borderline Pathfinders: The 1765 Diaries of Juan Maria Antonio de Rivera.* Ann Arbor, Michigan: University Microfilms International, 1991.

Lindgren, Raymond E., ed. "A Diary of Kit Carson's Navaho Campaign, 1863–1864," *New Mexico Historical Review* 21 (July 1946): 226–46.

Lingenfelter, Richard E. *Steamboats on the Colorado River, 1852–1916.* Tucson, Arizona: University of Arizona Press, 1978.

Marston, Otis. "Those Names in the Cave," *Desert* 14 (June 1951): 23.

Martin, Reed. Personal communication, 10 May 2000.

McClintock, James H. *Mormon Settlement in Arizona: A Record of Peaceful Conquest of the Desert.* New York: AMS Press, Inc., 1971.

McCormick, J. A. "The Colorado Grand Canon Mining & Improvement Company Expedition of 1891." Special Collections. Colorado School of Mines Library, Golden.

McElprang, Stella, ed. *"Castle Valley": A History of Emery County.* No city: Emery County Company of the Daughters of Utah Pioneers, 1949.

McKee, Edwin D. "Kanab Canyon: The Trail of Scientists," *Plateau* 18 (January 1946): 38–42.

McNitt, Frank. *Navajo Wars: Military Campaigns, Slave Raids, and Reprisals.* Albuquerque: University of New Mexico Press, 1972.

———. *Richard Wetherill: Anasazi.* Albuquerque: University of New Mexico Press, 1966.

McNitt, Frank, ed. *Navaho Expedition: Journal of a Military Reconnaissance from Santa Fe, New Mexico, to the Navaho Country, Made in 1849 by Lieutenant James H. Simpson.* Norman: University of Oklahoma Press, 1964.

McPherson, Robert S. *A History of San Juan County: In the Palm of Time.* Salt Lake City: Utah State Historical Society, 1995.

Mearns, Edgar A. "Field Notes." 1884. Files. National Museum of Natural History, Washington, D.C.

Menkes, Dove. Personal communication, 9 June 1992.

Mertz, Henriette. *Pale Ink: Two Ancient Records of Chinese Explorations in America.* Chicago: The Swallow Press, Inc., 1972.

Miller, David E. *Hole-In-The-Rock: An Epic in the Colonization of the Great American West.* Salt Lake City: University of Utah Press, 1966.

Miller, Hack. "Julius F. Stone, Frazier to Re-run Part of Colorado," *The Deseret News* (September 20, 1938).

"Minutes," *The Deseret News* (May 28, 1873).

Moore, William Haas. *Chiefs, Agents and Soldiers: Conflict on the Navajo Frontier, 1868–1882.* Albuquerque: University of New Mexico Press, 1994.

Moorehead, Warren K. "Field Diary of an Archeological Collector." Files. Ohio Historical Society, Columbus.

———. "In Search of a Lost Race," *The Illustrated American* (July 23, 1892): 457–60.

———. "In Search of a Lost Race," *The Illustrated American* (July 30, 1892): 511–14.

Murphy, Miriam B. *A History of Wayne County.* Salt Lake City: Utah State Historical Society, 1999.

Newell, Linda King, and Vivian Linford Talbot. *A History of Garfield County.* Salt Lake City: Utah State Historical Society, 1998.

Nossaman, Allen. Personal communication, 18 August 1993.

"Nothing of Note Comes from Navajo Mountain," *Rocky Mountain News* (April 3, 1882).

Olsen, Jr., Robert W. "Pipe Spring, Arizona, and Thereabouts," *The Journal of Arizona History* 6 (Spring 1965): 11–20.

Pace, William B. "Diary of William B. Pace During the Elk Mountain Mission, 1855–1856." Special Collections. Brigham Young University Library, Provo, Utah.

Patterson, Richard. *Butch Cassidy: A Biography.* Lincoln: University of Nebraska Press, 1998.

Perkins, Cornelia Adams, Marion Gardner Nielson, and Lenora Butt Jones. *Saga of San Juan.* No city: San Juan County Daughters of Utah Pioneers, 1968.

Peterson, Charles S. *Look to the Mountains: Southeastern Utah and the La Sal National Forest.* Provo, Utah: Brigham Young University Press, 1975.

———. *Take Up Your Mission: Mormon Colonizing Along the Little Colorado River, 1870–1900.* Tucson, Arizona: University of Arizona Press, 1973.

Phillips, Ann. "Archeological Expeditions into Southeastern Utah and Southwestern Colorado Between 1888–1898." In *Anasazi Basketmaker: Papers from the 1990 Wetherill–Grand Gulch Symposium,* edited by Victoria M. Atkins. Cultural Resources Series No. 24. Salt Lake City, Utah: Bureau of Land Management, 1993.

Powell, J. W. *Exploration of the Colorado River of the West and Its Tributaries. Explored in 1869, 1870, 1871, and 1872, Under the Direction of the Secretary of the Smithsonian Institution.* Washington: U.S. Government Printing Office, 1875.

Powell, Martin Clark. "A Study and Historical

Analysis of the Document 'The Trail of Hosteen Pish La Ki for Sixty Snows.'" 1963. M.S. thesis. University of Redlands Library, Redlands, California.

"A Prospecting Party Goes to Monumental Valley," *Rocky Mountain News* (May 23, 1882).

Redd, Charles. "Short Cut to San Juan." In *The 1949 Brand Book,* by Denver Posse of The Westerners. Fifth Annual Volume. Boulder, Colorado: Johnson Publishing Company, 1950.

Reid, H. Lorenzo. *Dixie of the Desert.* Zion National Park, Utah: Zion Natural History Association, 1964.

Reilly, P. T. *Lee's Ferry: From Mormon Crossing to National Park.* Logan, Utah: Utah State University Press, 1999.

Rhoades, Gale R., and Kerry Ross Boren. *Footprints in the Wilderness: A History of the Lost Rhoades Mines.* Salt Lake City, Utah: Dream Garden Press, 1980.

Richardson, Gladwell. *Navajo Trader.* Tucson: University of Arizona Press, 1986.

Robinson, Adonis Findlay, ed. *History of Kane County.* Salt Lake City, Utah: The Utah Printing Company, 1970.

Scorup, Stena. *J. A. Scorup: A Utah Cattleman.* Privately printed, no date.

Shlaer, Robert. *Sights Once Seen: Daguerreotyping Fremont's Last Expedition through the Rockies.* Santa Fe: Museum of New Mexico Press, 2000.

Sibley, H. H. "Sibley to L. L. Rich, 12 November 1860." Letter, Records of Army Commands. National Archives and Records Service, Washington, D.C.

Silliman, Bert J. "The Orejas del Oso Trail, or Bear's Ears Trail." Silliman Papers. Utah State Historical Society, Salt Lake City.

Slater, John M. *El Morro: Inscription Rock, New Mexico.* Los Angeles: The Plantin Press, 1961.

Smart, Donna T. "Over the Rim to Red Rock Country: The Parley Pratt Exploring Company of 1849," *Utah Historical Quarterly* 62 (Spring 1994): 171–90.

Smith, Duane A. *Mesa Verde National Park: Shadows of the Centuries.* Lawrence, Kansas: University Press of Kansas, 1988.

Smith, Dwight L., ed. *Down the Colorado: Robert Brewster Stanton.* Norman: University of Oklahoma Press, 1965.

———. *The Photographer and the River, 1889–90: The Colorado River Diary of Franklin A. Nims.* San Francisco: Stagecoach Press, 1967.

Smith, Dwight L., and C. Gregory Crampton, eds. *The Colorado River Survey: Robert B. Stanton and the Denver, Colorado Canon and Pacific Railroad.* Salt Lake City and Chicago: Howe Brothers, 1987.

Snow, Anne, ed. *Rainbow Views: A History of Wayne County.* Springville, Utah: Art City Publishing Company, 1977.

Solomon, William H. "Arizona Mission." 1874. Special Collections. University of Utah Library, Salt Lake City.

Sorgenfrei, Robert. "'A Fortune Awaits Enterprise Here': The Best Mining Expedition to the Grand Canyon in 1891," *Journal of the Southwest* 40 (Winter 1998): 437–62.

Standifird, John Henry. "Journal of John Henry

Standifird, Vol. I." 1873. Special Collections. University of Utah Library, Salt Lake City.

Stanton, Robert B. "Steamboat Navigation," in "The River and the Canyon." Unpublished manuscript, Stanton Collection, New York Public Library.

———. "The River and the Canon: The Colorado River of the West and the Exploration, Navigation, and Survey of its Canons, from the Standpoint of an Engineer." Stanton Papers. New York Public Library.

Steen, Charlie R. "The Natural Bridges of White Canyon: A Diary of H. L. A. Culmer, 1905," *Utah Historical Quarterly* 40 (Winter 1972): 55–87.

Stegner, Wallace. *Beyond the Hundredth Meridian: John Wesley Powell and the Second Opening of the West*. Boston: Houghton Mifflin Company, 1954.

Stiles, Helen J., ed. "Down the Colorado in 1889," *The Colorado Magazine* 41 (Summer 1964): 225–46.

Tanner, Faun McConkie. *The Far Country: A Regional History of Moab and La Sal, Utah*. Salt Lake City, Utah: Olympus Publishing Company, 1976.

Taylor, Samuel. Personal communication, 18 September 1986.

Thompson, George A. *Lost Treasures on the Old Spanish Trail*. Salt Lake City, Utah: Western Epics, 1986.

Tippetts, Ruby Noyes. *A Song in Her Heart*. Privately printed, 1961.

Topping, Gary. *Glen Canyon and the San Juan Country*. Moscow, Idaho: University of Idaho Press, 1997.

Trafzer, Clifford E. *The Kit Carson Campaign: The Last Great Navajo War*. Norman: University of Oklahoma Press, 1982.

"Up from Colorado Canon," *The Denver Republican* (July 17, 1892).

Van Cott, John W. *Utah Place Names: A Comprehensive Guide to the Origins of Geographic Names*. Salt Lake City, Utah: University of Utah Press, 1990.

Van Valkenburgh, Richard. "Inscription at Hwoye Spring." *Desert* 4 (January 1941): 9–11.

———. *Navajo Country, Dine Bikeyah: A Geographical Dictionary of Navajo Lands in the 1930s*. Mancos, Colorado: Time Traveler Maps, 1999.

Verkamp, Margaret M. *History of Grand Canyon National Park*. Flagstaff, Arizona: Grand Canyon Pioneers Society, 1993.

Walcott, Charles D. "Report of Charles D. Walcott," in *Fourth Annual Report of the United States Geological Survey, 1882–'83*. Washington: U.S. Government Printing Office, 1884.

Ward, Albert E. *Inscription House: Two Research Reports*. Technical Series No. 16. Flagstaff, Arizona: Museum of Northern Arizona, 1975.

Warner, Ted J., ed. *The Dominguez-Escalante Journal: Their Expedition through Colorado, Utah, Arizona, and New Mexico in 1776*. Salt Lake City: University of Utah Press, 1995.

Webb, Roy. *Call of the Colorado*. Moscow, Idaho: University of Idaho Press, 1994.

Webb, Roy. *If We Had a Boat: Green River Explorers, Adventurers, and Runners*. Salt Lake City: University of Utah Press, 1986.

Weber, David J. *The Taos Trappers: The Fur Trade in the Far Southwest, 1540–1846.* Norman: University of Oklahoma Press, 1971.

Wetherill, John. "Navajo National Monument," *The Southwestern Monuments Monthly Report* (March 1934): 2–6.

Williams, Joseph. *Narrative of a Tour from the State of Indiana to the Oregon Territory, in the Years 1841–42.* Cincinnati: J. B. Wilson, Printer, 1843.

Wilson, Iris Higbee. *William Wolfskill, 1798–1866.* Glendale, California: The Arthur H. Clark Company, 1965.

Winship, George Parker, ed. *The Journey of Coronado, 1540–1542.* Golden, Colorado: Fulcrum Publishing, 1990.

Wixom, Hartt. *A Modern Look at the Frontier Life and Legend of Jacob Hamblin.* Springville, Utah: Cedar Fort, Inc., 1996.

Woolsey, Nethella Griffin. *The Escalante Story: A History of the Town of Escalante, and Description of the Surrounding Territory, Garfield County, Utah, 1875–1964.* Springville, Utah: Art City Publishing Company, 1964.

Worster, Donald. *A River Running West: The Life of John Wesley Powell.* New York: Oxford University Press, 2001.

Index